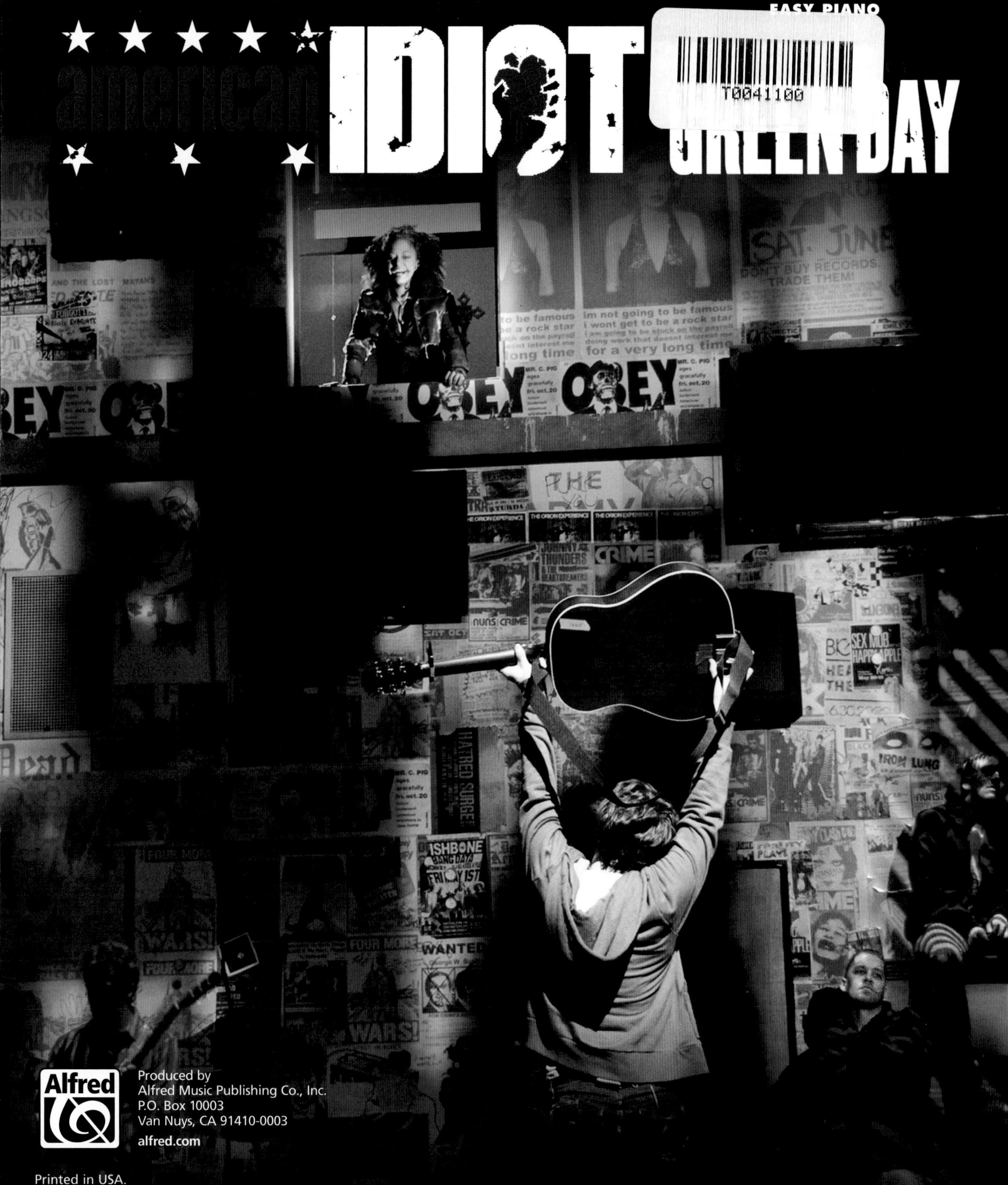

Produced by
Alfred Music Publishing Co., Inc.
P.O. Box 10003
Van Nuys, CA 91410-0003
alfred.com

Printed in USA.

ISBN-10: 0-7390-7317-6
ISBN-13: 978-0-7390-7317-9

Photography: Doug Hamilton, Page 6 Kevin Berne

Alfred Cares. Contents printed on 100% recycled paper, except pages 1–8 which are printed on 60% recycled paper.

BLESSED

OBEY OBEY OBEY OBEY OBEY
RUTHIE'S INN
SAT JUNE 30 9PM

CONTENTS

Tom Hulce & Ira Pittelman

Ruth and Stephen Hendel   Vivek J. Tiwary and Gary Kaplan   Aged In Wood and Burnt Umber
Scott M. Delman   Latitude Link   HOP Theatricals and Jeffrey Finn   Larry Welk
Bensinger Filerman and Moellenberg Taylor   Allan S. Gordon and Élan V. McAllister
Berkeley Repertory Theatre

In Association with
Awaken Entertainment   John Pinckard and John Domo

Present

american IDIOT

Music by
Green Day

Lyrics by
Billie Joe Armstrong

Book by
Billie Joe Armstrong and Michael Mayer

John Gallagher Jr.
Stark Sands   Michael Esper
Rebecca Naomi Jones   Christina Sajous   Mary Faber
and
Tony Vincent

with

Declan Bennett   Andrew Call   Gerard Canonico   Miguel Cervantes   Joshua Henry   Van Hughes
Brian Charles Johnson   Joshua Kobak   Omar Lopez-Cepero   Leslie McDonel
Chase Peacock   Theo Stockman   Ben Thompson   Alysha Umphress   Aspen Vincent   Libby Winters

Scenic Design
Christine Jones

Costume Design
Andrea Lauer

Lighting Design
Kevin Adams

Sound Design
Brian Ronan

Video/Projection Design
Darrel Maloney

Casting
Jim Carnahan, C.S.A.
Carrie Gardner, C.S.A.

Production Stage Manager
James Harker

Vocal Coach
Liz Caplan Vocal Studios, LLC

Music Coordinator
Michael Keller

General Management
Abbie M. Strassler

Technical Supervisor
Hudson Theatrical Associates

Press Representative
The Hartman Group

Marketing
Type A Marketing

Music Director
Carmel Dean

Associate Choreographer
Lorin Latarro

Associate Director
Johanna McKeon

Associate Producers
SenovvA   Lee Marshall   Tracy Straus and Barney Straus   Lorenzo Thione and Jay Kuo
Pat Magnarella   Christopher Maring

Musical Supervision, Arrangements, and Orchestrations
Tom Kitt

Choreographer
Steven Hoggett

Director
Michael Mayer

World Premiere produced by Berkeley Repertory Theatre, September 2009
Tony Taccone, Artistic Director   Susan Medak, Managing Director

AMERICAN IDIOT SYNOPSIS

Prologue: Dozens of televisions announce random bits of news, gossip, and commercials. Everyone is fixated on his or her own television. Fed up with the state of the union, the company explodes in anger ("American Idiot"). We find ourselves in a suburban wasteland at some point in the recent past. We meet JOHNNY. He's almost 30 and he's done nothing with his life. He goes to commiserate with his friend WILL ("Jesus of Suburbia"). Their friend TUNNY shows up, and they party. When the three of them run out of beer, they head to the 7-II, where TUNNY exposes the do-nothing go-nowhere quicksand of their lives ("City of the Damned"). They get riled up, and JOHNNY challenges his friends to give a shit. ("I Don't Care"). HEATHER appears. She is pregnant, and doesn't know what to do ("Dearly Beloved"). Meanwhile, a decision is made. JOHNNY, WILL, and TUNNY will head to The City to start a new life. At the last moment, HEATHER reveals to WILL that she is pregnant with his child - and WILL decides to stay home ("Tales From Another Broken Home").

JOHNNY and TUNNY take a bus across the country. As expected, the America they find sickens them, and they redouble their commitment to forging their own path ("Holiday"). They arrive in The City and share a cheap room at a dive hotel. Days pass. TUNNY sleeps, but JOHNNY walks out into the night to claim his connection to the city. He even sees a lonely girl in a window and flirts with her ("Boulevard Of Broken Dreams"). Back in the hotel, TUNNY wakes up. Disillusioned with the city, he has a television-induced mystical revelation ("Favorite Son"). Mesmerizing images of power and patriotism inspire TUNNY to enlist in the military. ("Are We The Waiting"). JOHNNY returns to the hotel to find TUNNY gone. Alone and desperate, JOHNNY conjures an all-powerful alter ego, ST. JIMMY. Surrounded by disciples and jacked up on ST. JIMMY'S charisma and drugs, JOHNNY tracks down the girl in the window, WHATSERNAME, and makes his move ("St. Jimmy").

JOHNNY hooks up with WHATSERNAME. Back in suburbia, WILL and HEATHER struggle to keep their relationship alive, but WILL's inertia threatens to get the best of him. Meanwhile, in the Middle East, we find TUNNY in combat, where he is injured ("Give Me Novocaine"). JOHNNY is smitten with WHATSERNAME and wants to celebrate, but ST. JIMMY has other plans for them ("Last Of The American Girls / She's A Rebel"). ST. JIMMY gives JOHNNY and WHATSERNAME some high-grade heroin, and they shoot up. By this time, WILL and HEATHER 's baby has been born, and WILL is increasingly oblivious as HEATHER tenderly commits herself to her baby's future ("Last Night On Earth"). HEATHER has had enough of WILL's pot-and-alcohol-fueled apathy. Despite WILL's protestations, she takes the baby and walks out ("Too Much Too Soon").

TUNNY is in a military hospital in the Middle East with three other injured soldiers ("Before The Lobotomy"). His left leg has been severely wounded. In a morphine-induced hallucination, a mysterious burqa-clad seductress appears to him from the sky. She pulls him into an ecstatic mid-air dance. ("Extraordinary Girl").

The mirage disappears and he is left with his fellow soldiers in agony ("Before The Lobotomy (Reprise)"). In the city, JOHNNY sings WHATSERNAME a beautiful love song that he has written for her ("When It's Time"). This propels ST. JIMMY to action. Threatened by JOHNNY and WHATSERNAME's intensifying connection, he retaliates by trying to separate them. JOHNNY's need for drugs suddenly increases. As he ties off and shoots up, he pictures WILL, and they reiterate their old credo. ("Know Your Enemy").

Three simultaneous events: In the military hospital, TUNNY's leg has been amputated. His nurse, the EXTRAORDINARY GIRL from his fantasy, gives him a sponge bath and comforts him. Back in suburbia, WILL is alone, and HEATHER is somewhere far away, with their child. In the city, WHATSERNAME appeals to JOHNNY to clean up and get serious about his life and their relationship ("21 Guns"). JOHNNY can't handle it, and leaves under the continuing influence of ST. JIMMY. WHATSERNAME has had it, and she leaves JOHNNY ("Letterbomb"). JOHNNY hits rock bottom. He longs for better days ahead, TUNNY longs for home, and WILL longs for all the things he's lost ("Wake Me Up When September Ends").

JOHNNY commits to getting clean. ST. JIMMY realizes his days are numbered, and the JOHNNY/ST. JIMMY matrix explodes in the metaphorical suicide of ST. JIMMY ("The Death of St. Jimmy"). JOHNNY joins the work force. He doesn't like it so much ("East 12th St."). WILL, out of grass and all alone with his television, bemoans his outcast state. ("Nobody Likes You"). He finally gets up off the couch, when suddenly HEATHER appears on television with her new rockstar boyfriend. ("Rock and Roll Girlfriend"). WILL freaks. He heads to the 7-11, waiting for something to happen. JOHNNY returns home, and so does TUNNY. JOHNNY, TUNNY, and WILL reunite in the parking lot of the 7-11. TUNNY introduces his EXTRAORDINARY GIRL, who has returned home with him. HEATHER and her rock and roll boyfriend arrive. In an uneasy truce, she allows WILL to show his kid to his two best friends. Other friends show up, too, to greet the three guys who they haven't seen in a year ("We're Coming Home"). Epilogue: A year has gone by. JOHNNY reflects on the mistakes of his past. And for the first time he can live inside the struggle between rage and love that has defined his life. With this acceptance comes the possibility of hope ("Whatsername").

AMERICAN IDIOT

Words by Billie Joe
Music by Green Day
Arranged by Carol Matz

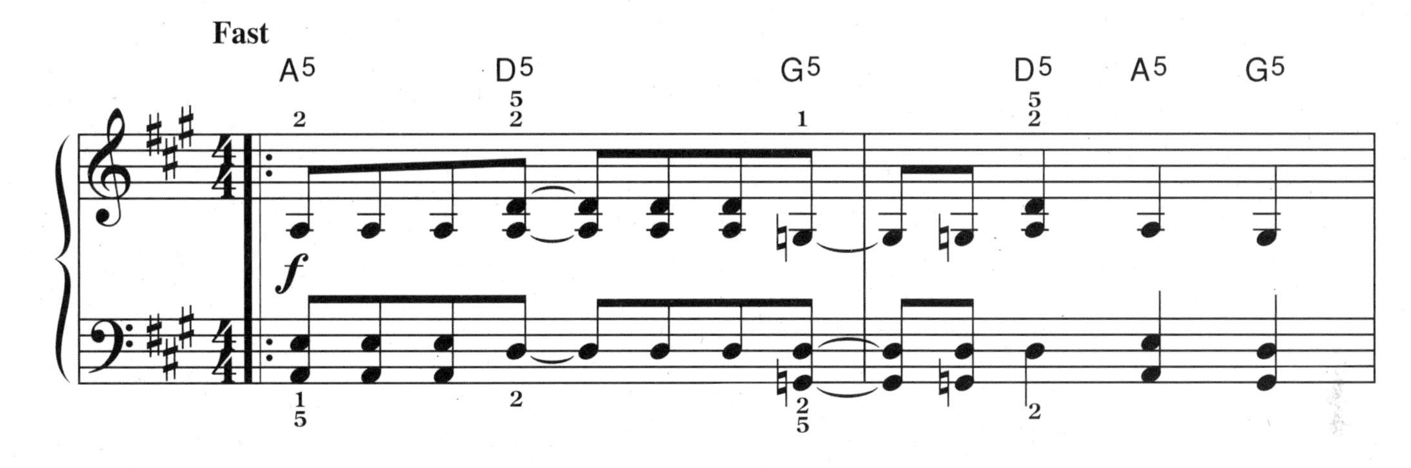

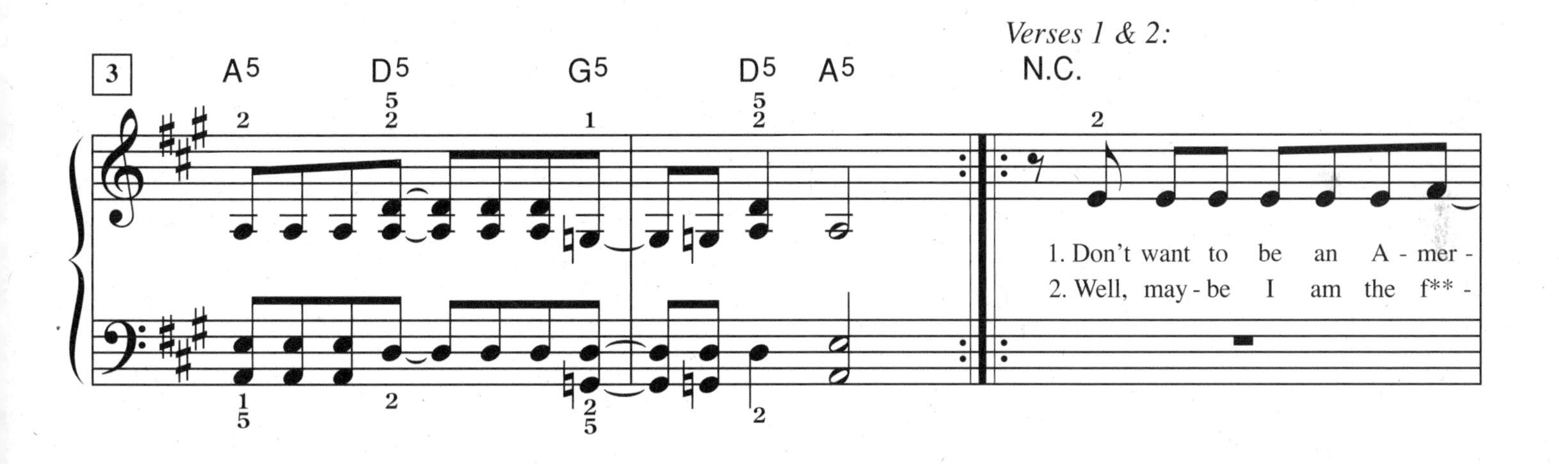

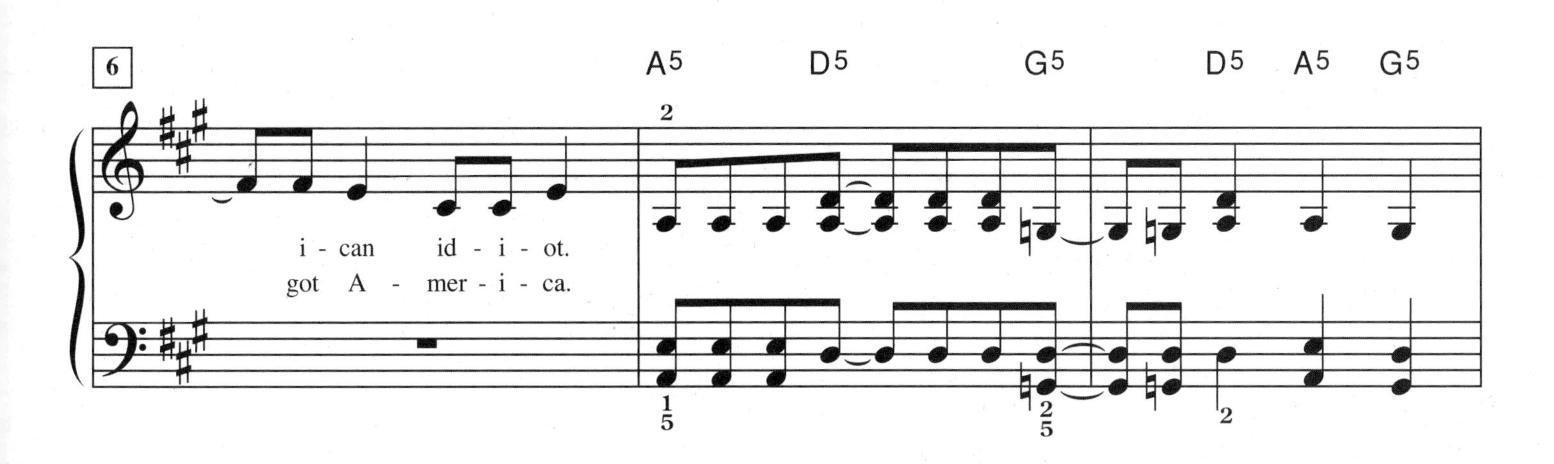

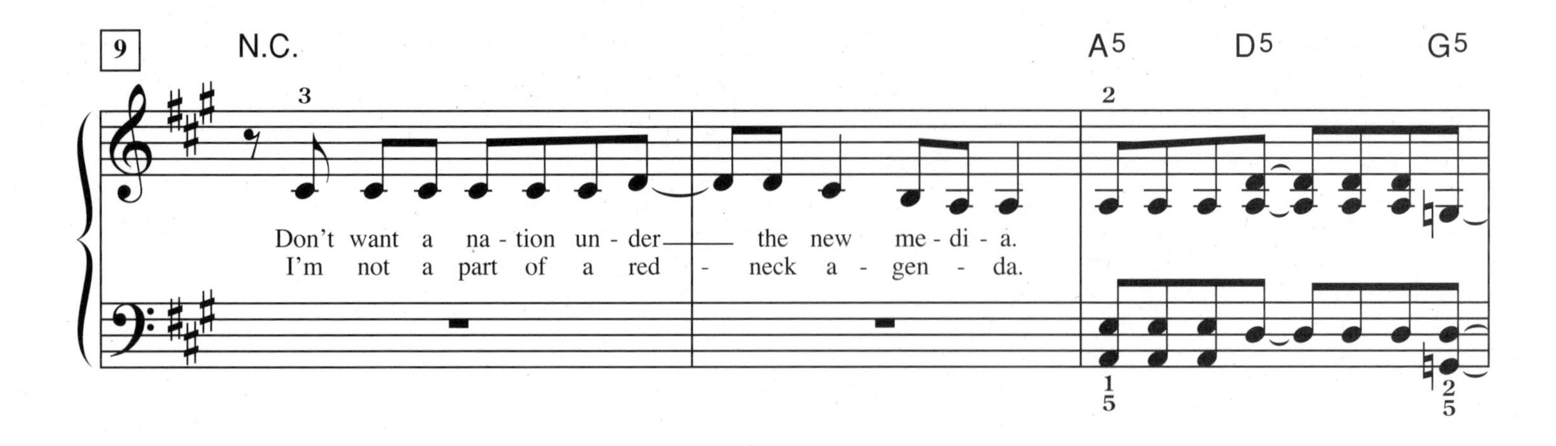
9
N.C.
A5 D5 G5
Don't want a na - tion un - der the new me - di - a.
I'm not a part of a red - neck a - gen - da.

12
D5 A5 N.C.
Hey, can you hear the sound of hys - ter - i - a?
Now, ev - 'ry - bod - y, do the prop - a - gan - da,

15
A5 D5 G5 D5 A5 G5 N.C.
The sub - lim - i - nal mind-
and sing along to the age

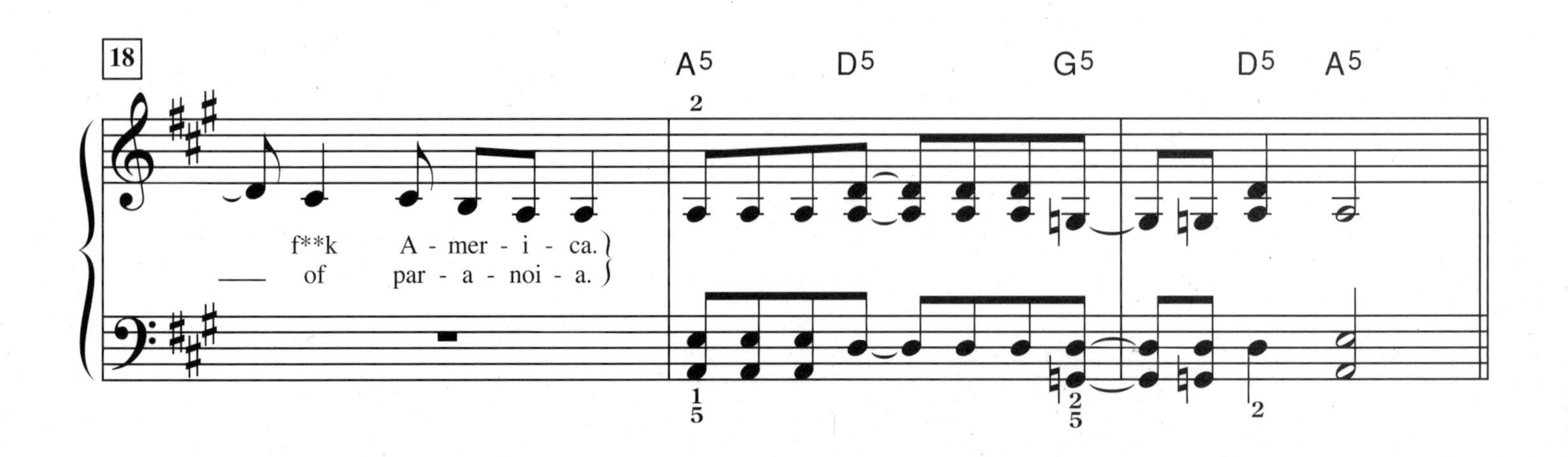
18
A5 D5 G5 D5 A5
f**k A - mer - i - ca.
of par - a - noi - a.

Chorus:
21
D
A
Wel-come to a new kind of ten - sion all a-cross the a -

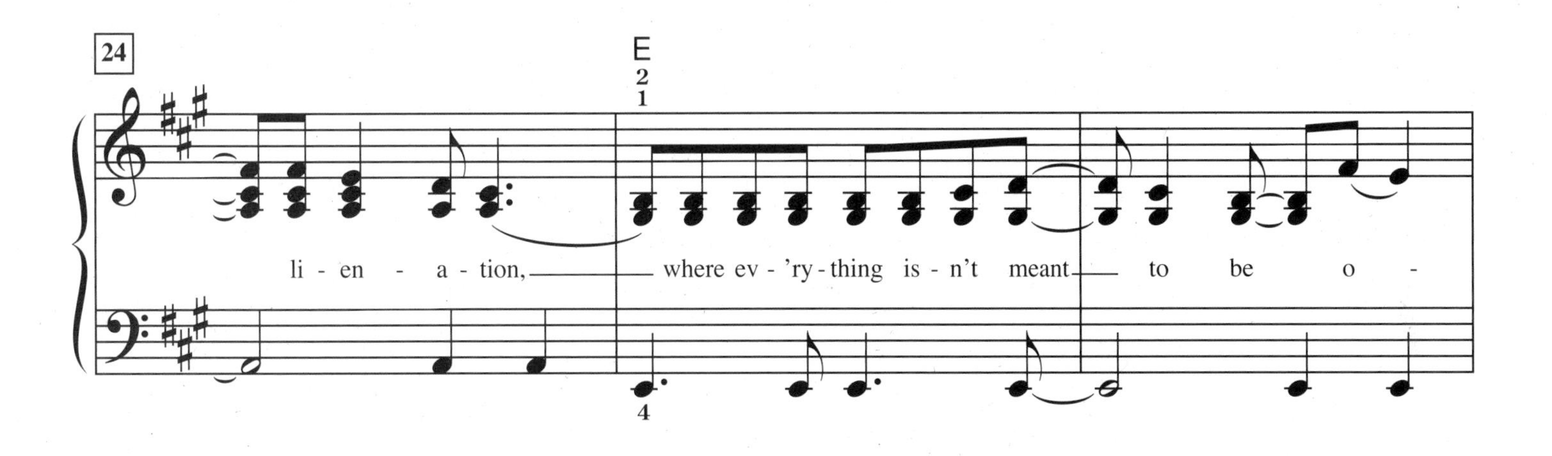
24
E
li - en - a - tion, where ev - 'ry-thing is - n't meant to be o -

27
A
D
kay.
Tel - e - vi - sion dreams

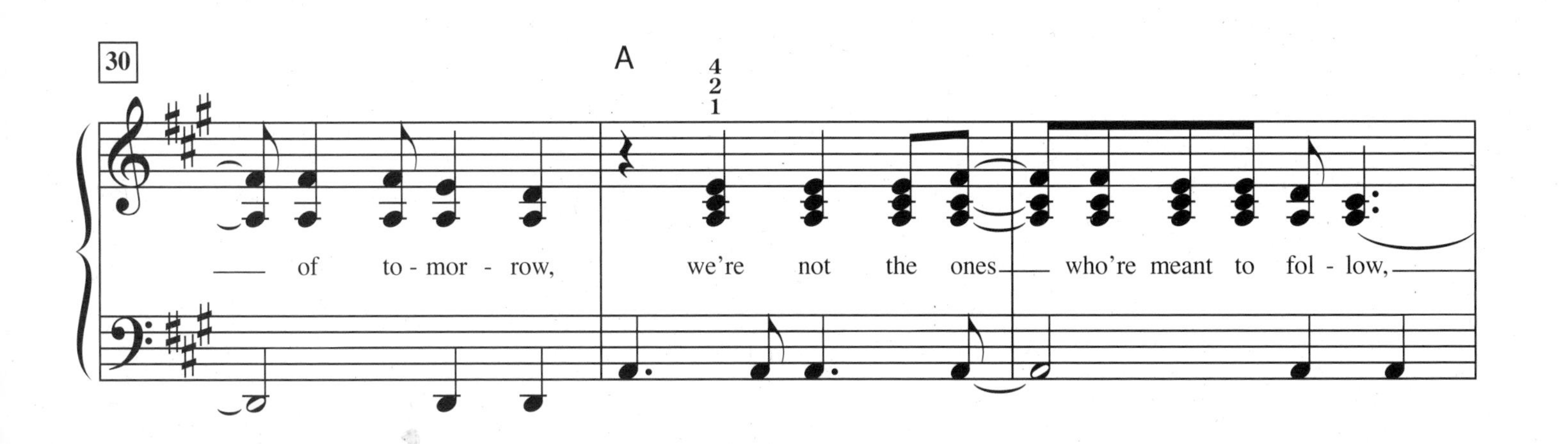
30
A
of to - mor - row, we're not the ones who're meant to fol - low,

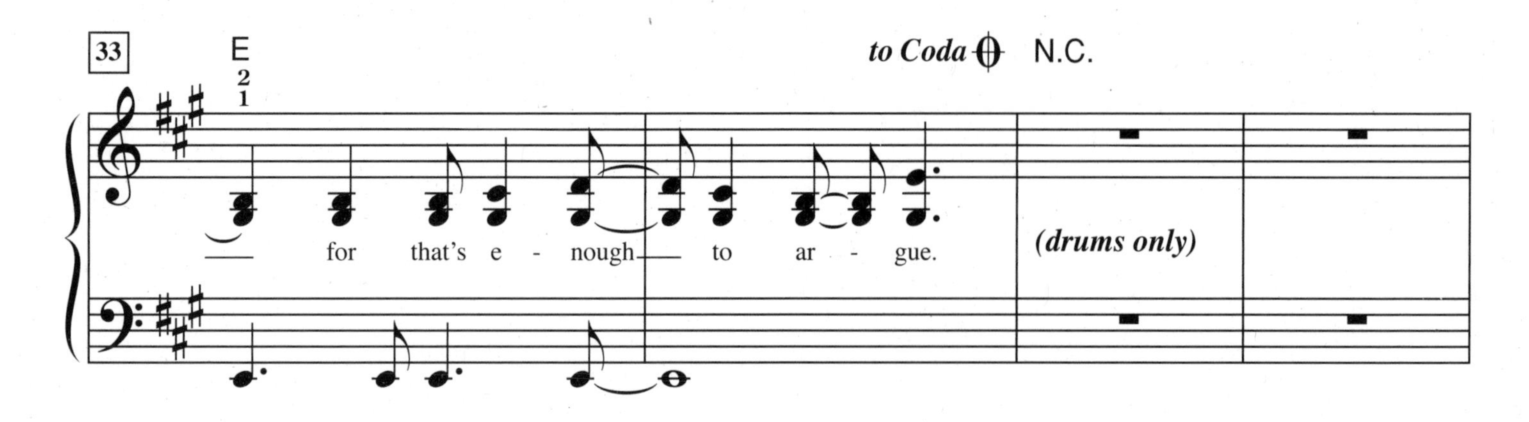
33
E
to Coda
N.C.
for that's e - nough to ar - gue.
(drums only)

37
A5 D5 G5 D5 A5 G5 A5 D5 G5

40
D5 A5
Verse 3:
D5 G5 D5 A5
3. Don't want to be an A - mer - i - can id - i - ot,

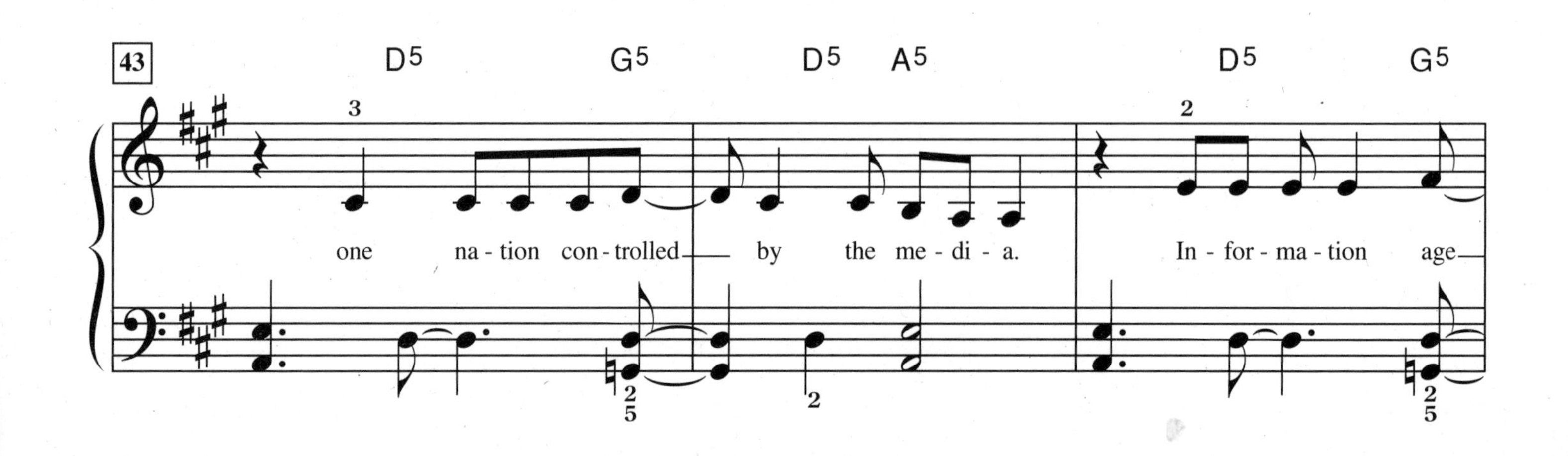
43
D5 G5 D5 A5 D5 G5
one na - tion con - trolled by the me - di - a. In - for - ma - tion age

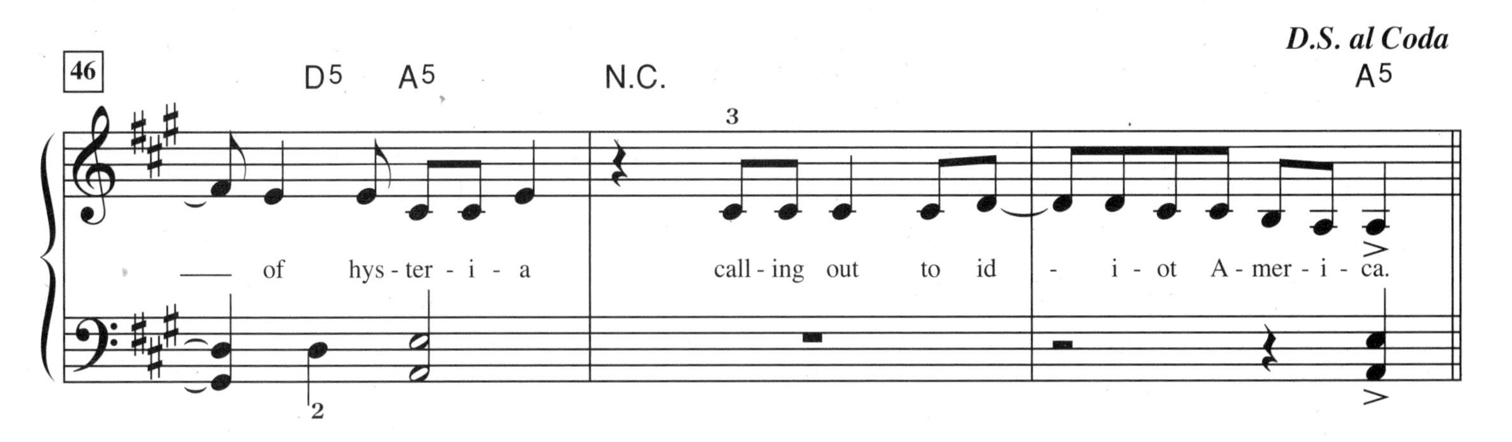
46
D.S. al Coda
D5 A5 N.C. A5
3
of hys - ter - i - a calling out to id - i - ot A - mer - i - ca.
2

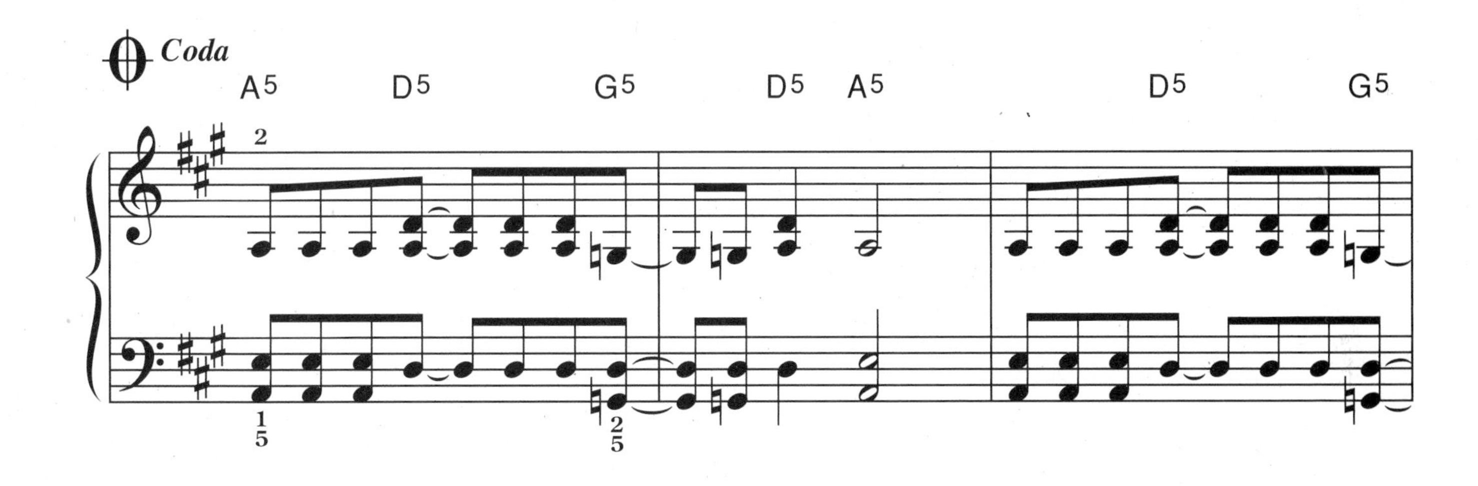
Coda
A5 D5 G5 D5 A5 D5 G5

52
D5 A5 G5 A5 D5 G5 D5 A5 D5 G5

56
D5 A5 G5 A5 D5 G5 D5 A5

HOLIDAY

Words by Billie Joe
Music by Green Day
Arranged by Carol Matz

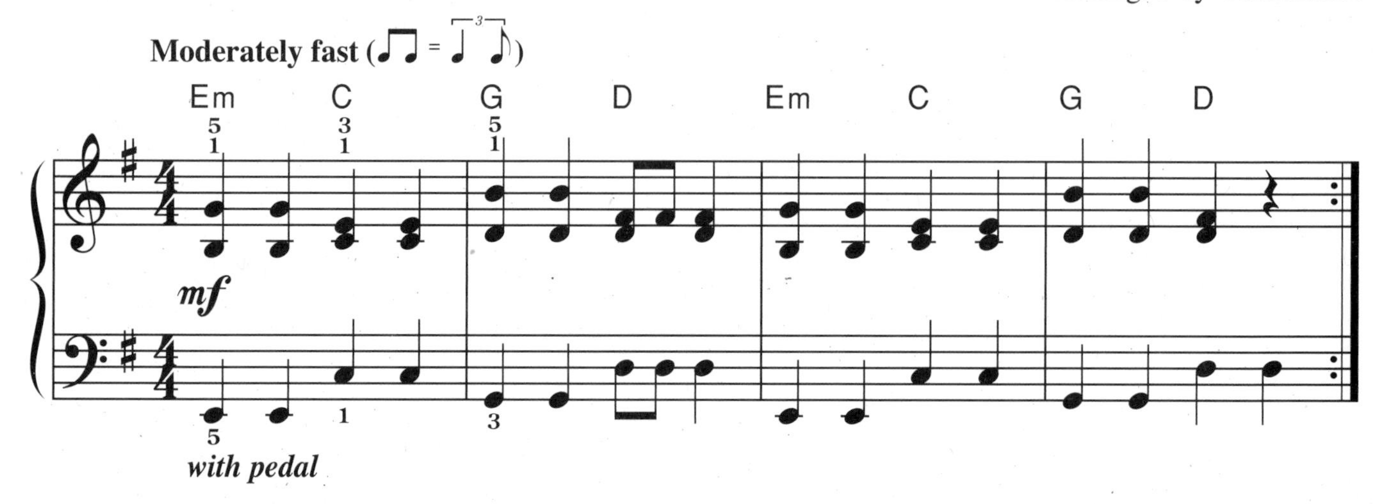

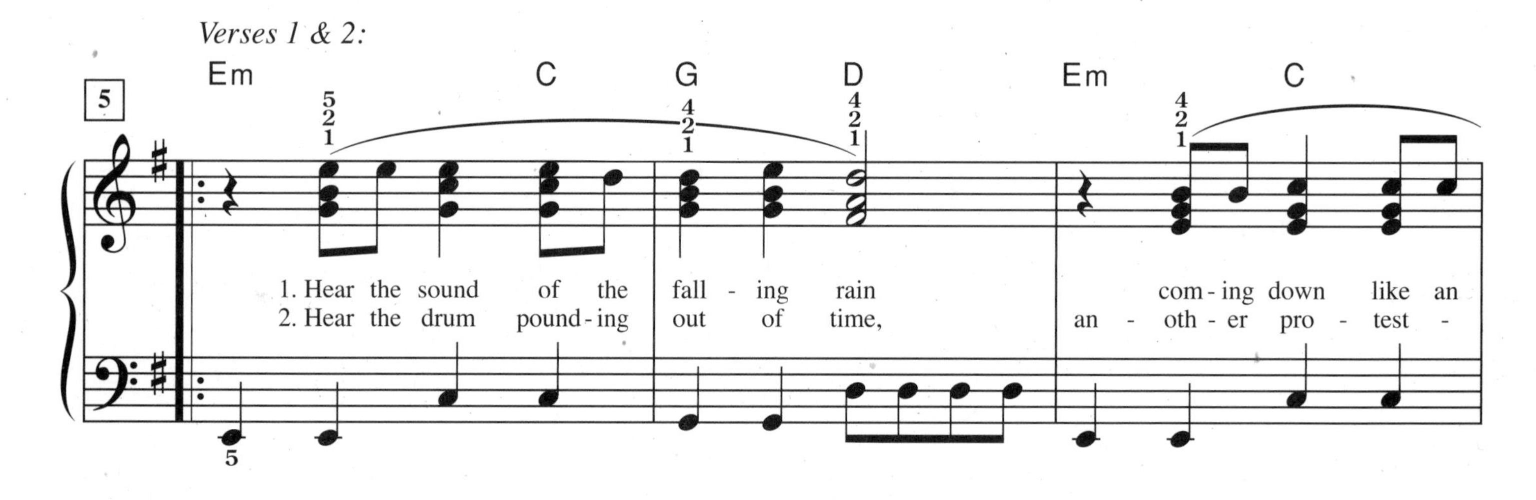

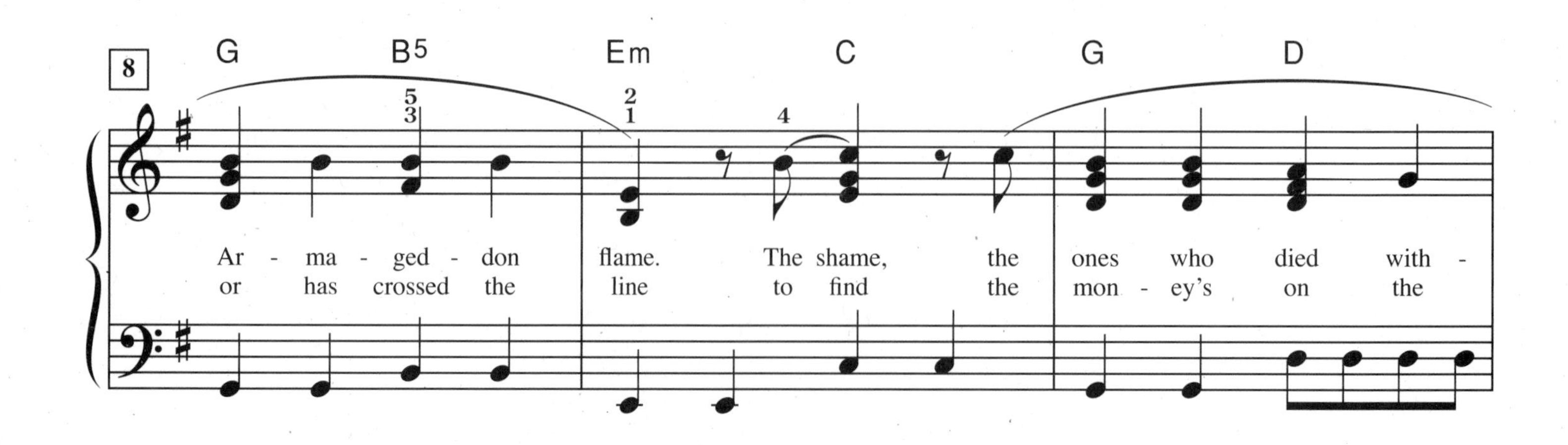

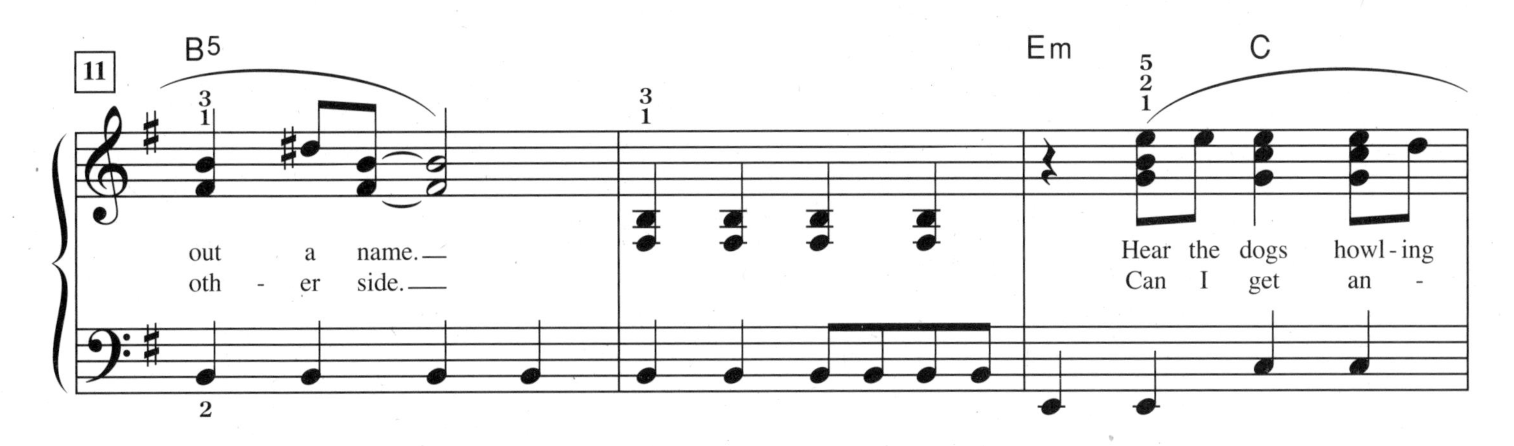
11
B5
Em
C
out a name.
oth - er side.
Hear the dogs howl - ing
Can I get an -

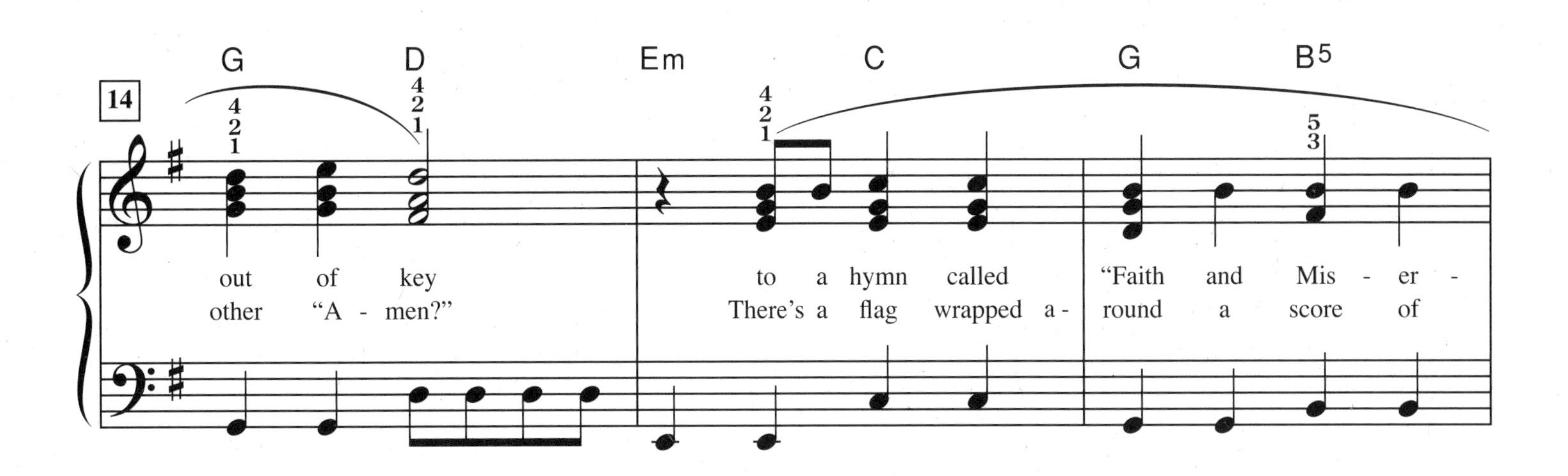
14
G
D
Em
C
G
B5
out of key
other "A - men?"
to a hymn called
There's a flag wrapped a -
"Faith and Mis - er -
round a score of

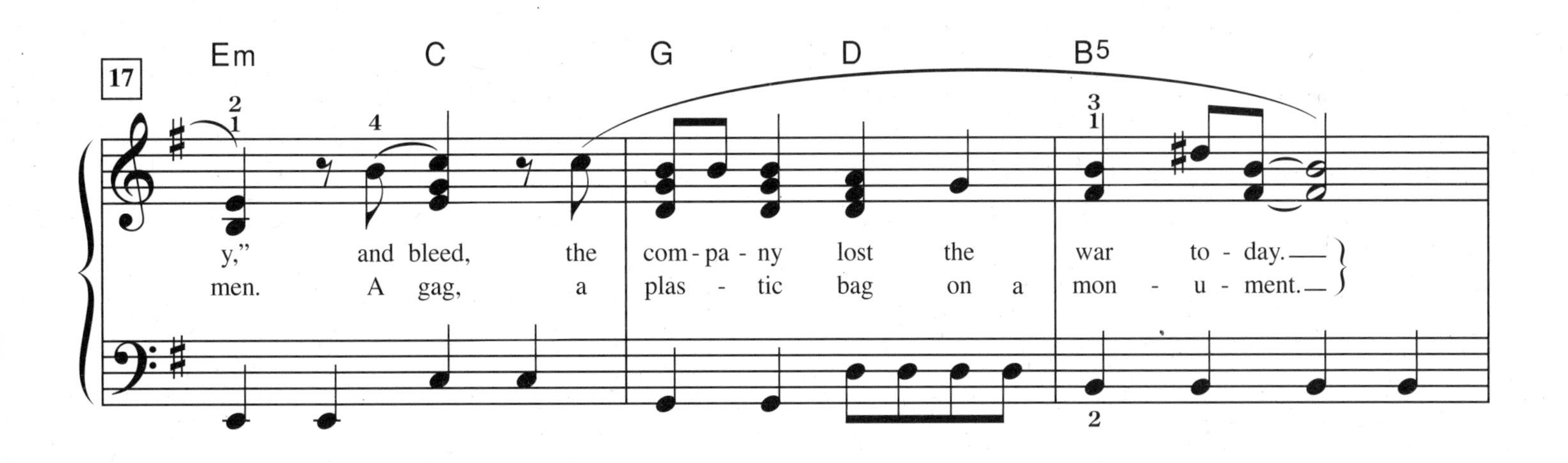
17
Em
C
G
D
B5
y," and bleed, the
men. A gag, a
com - pa - ny lost the
plas - tic bag on a
war to - day.
mon - u - ment.

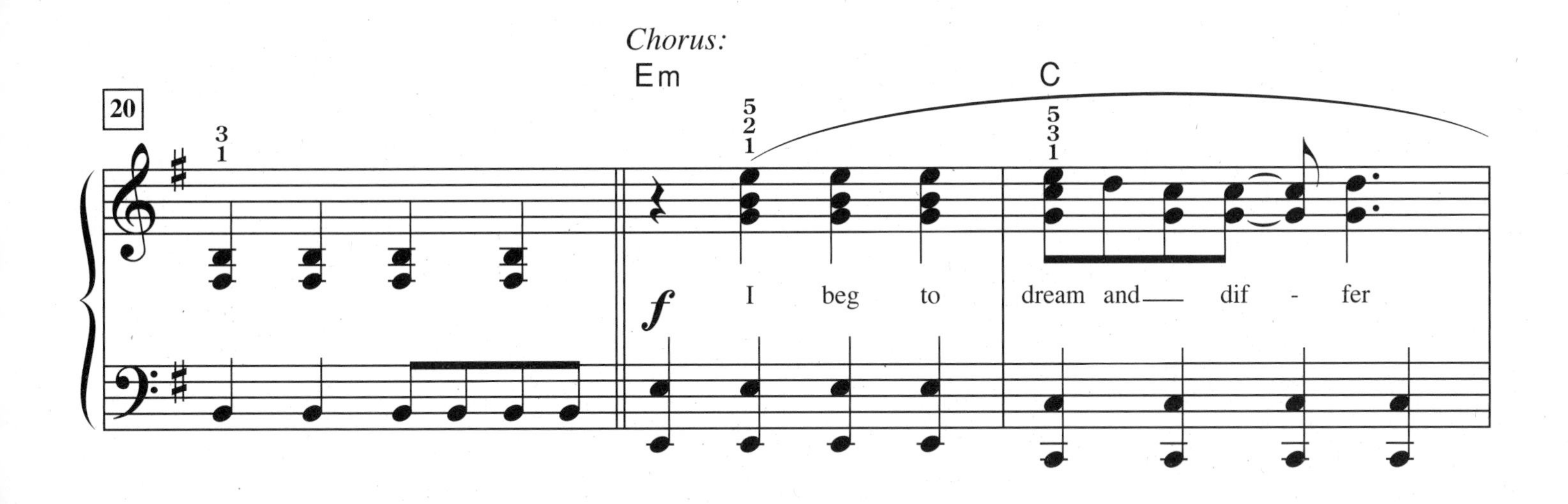
Chorus:
20
Em
C
I beg to
dream and dif - fer

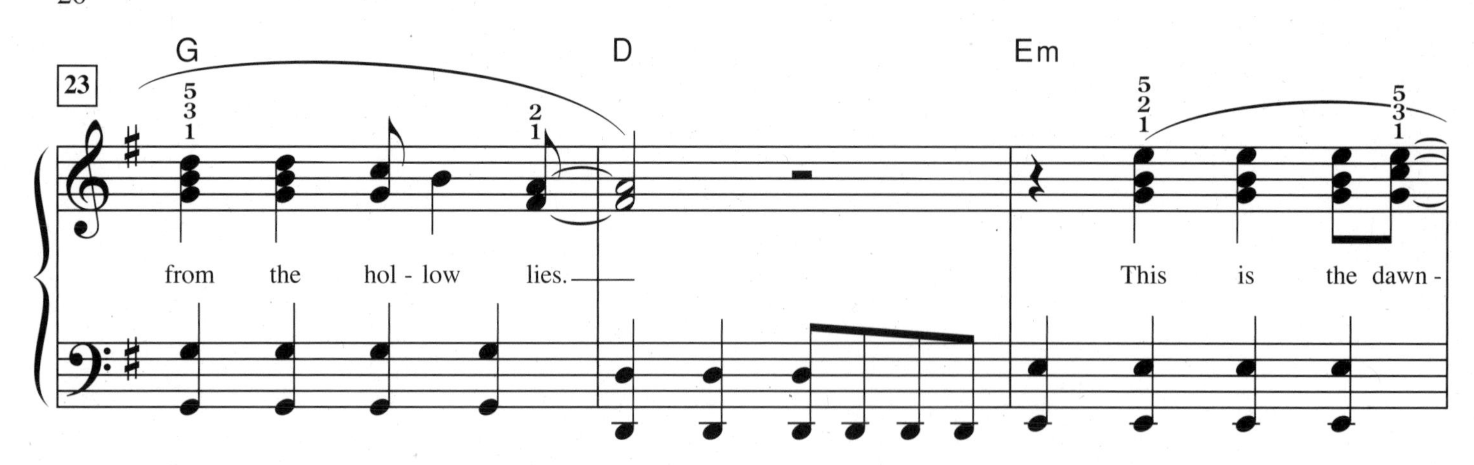
23
G
D
Em
from the hol - low lies.
This is the dawn -

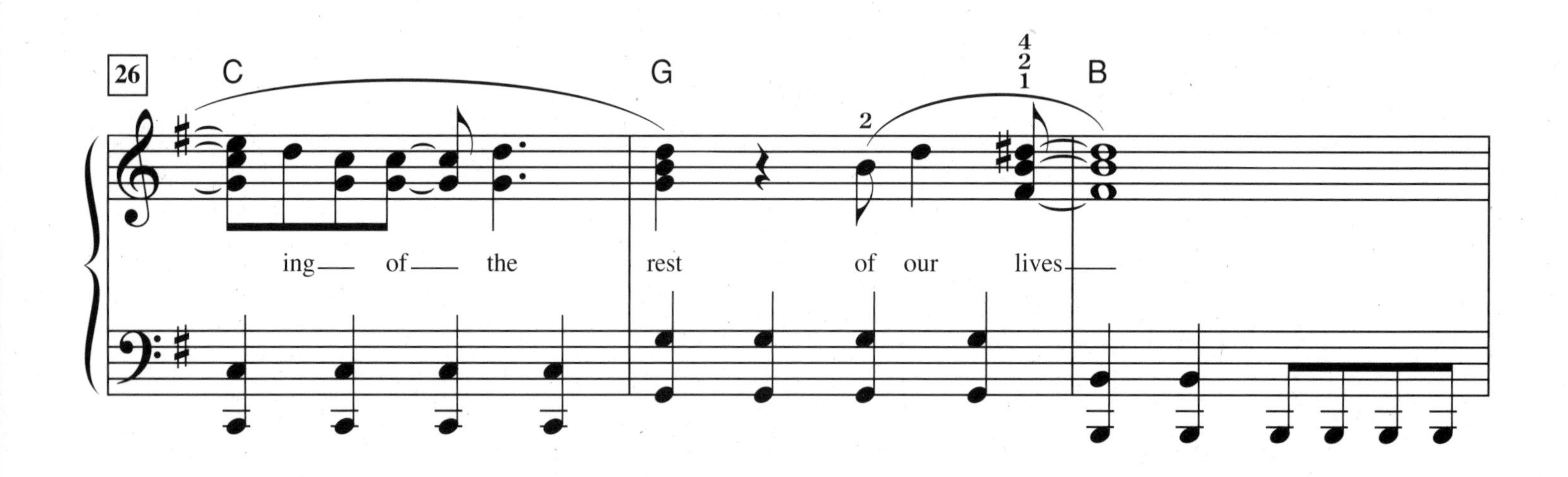
26
C
G
B
ing of the rest of our lives

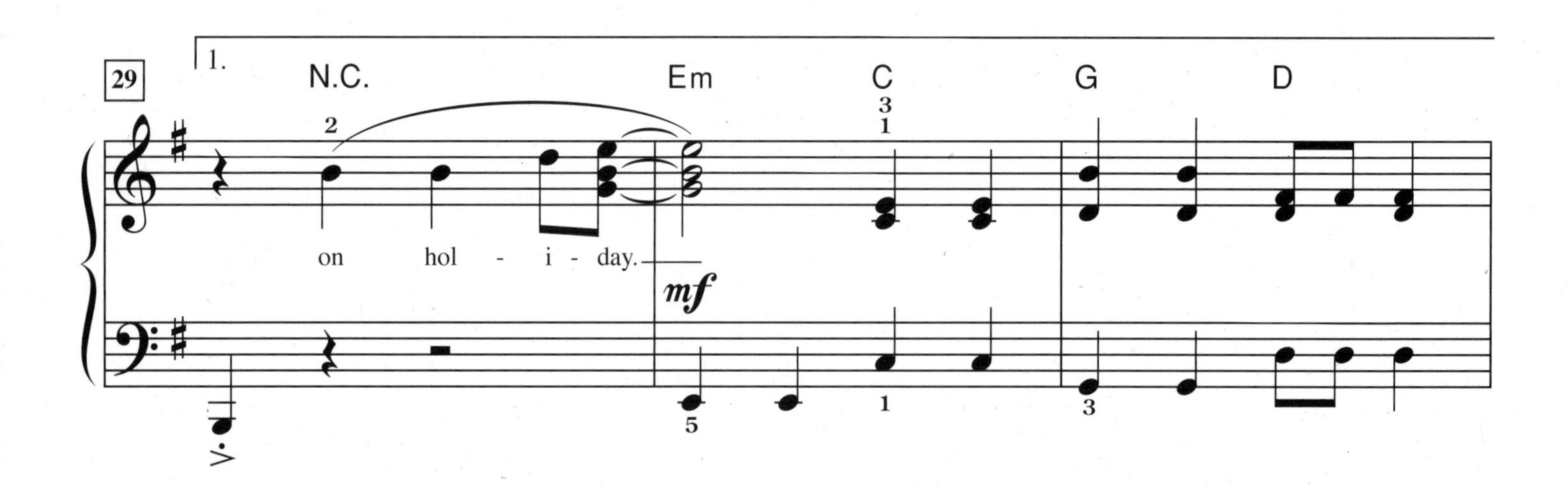
29
1.
N.C.
Em
C
G
D
on hol - i - day.
mf

32
Em
C
G
D
2.
N.C.
on hol - i - day.

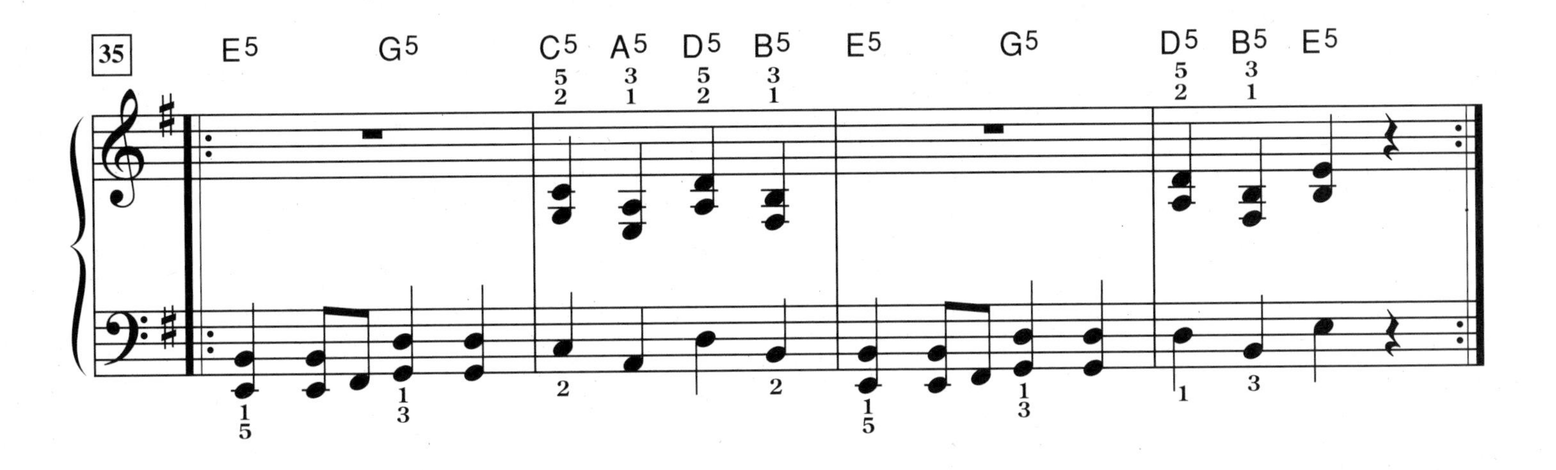
35
E5 G5 C5 A5 D5 B5 E5 G5 D5 B5 E5

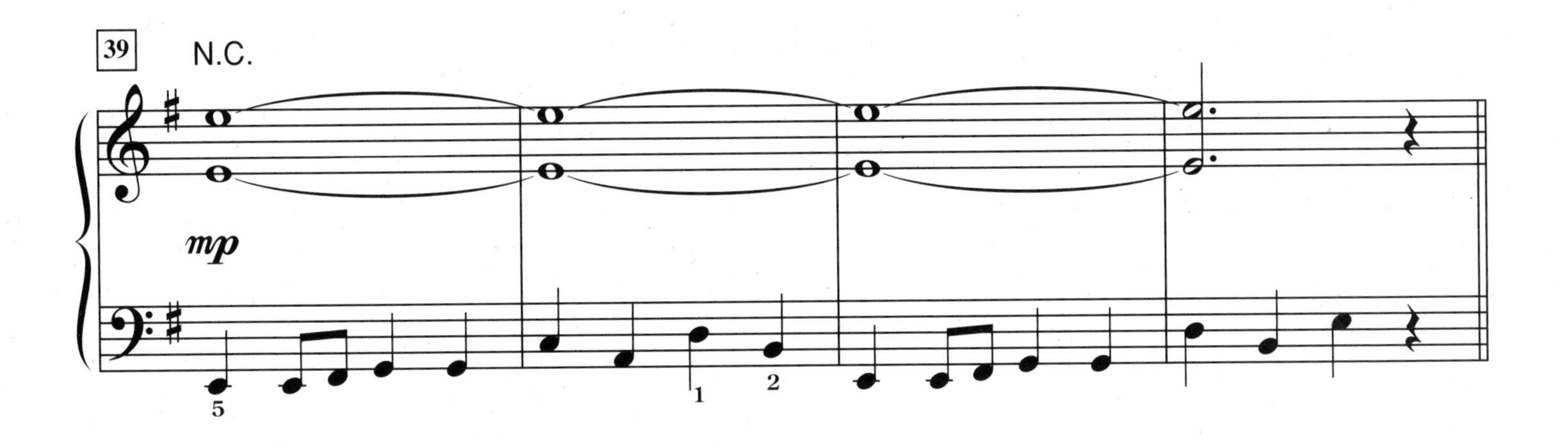
39
N.C.
mp

43
Bridge: Play 5 times
mf (See additional lyrics.)

47
B5
Just 'cause, just 'cause, be - cause we're out - laws, yeah.

Chorus:
Em
C
G
51
I beg to dream and dif - fer from the hol - low lies.
D
Em
C
54
This is the dawn - ing of the
G
1.
B
2.
B
57
rest of our lives.
60
This is our lives on hol - i - day.

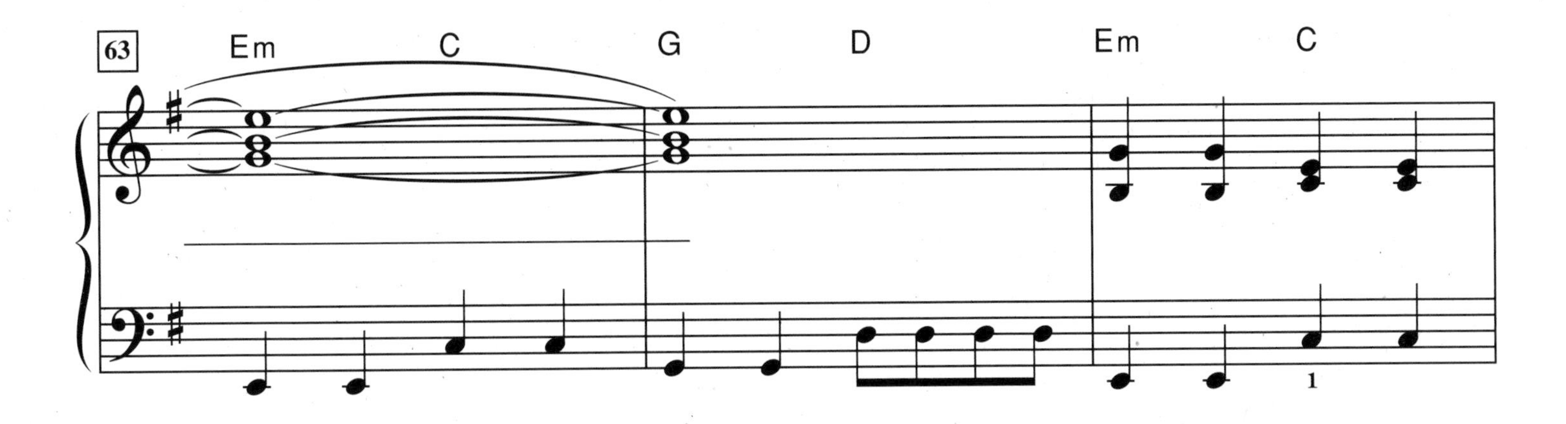

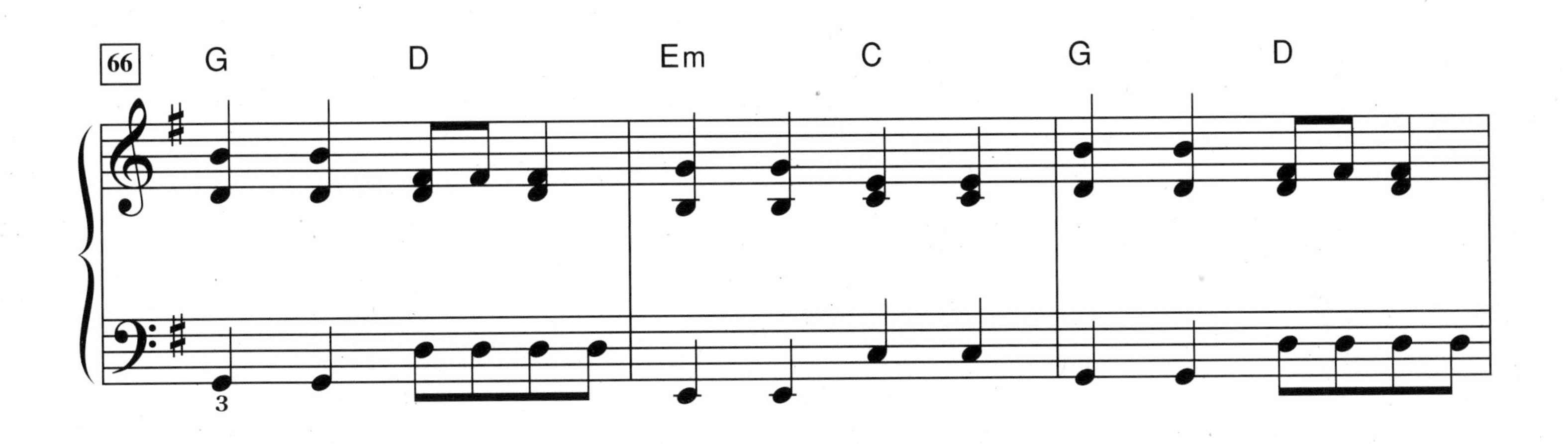

Bridge (spoken lyrics):
The representative from Jingletown has the floor.
Zieg Heil to the President gasman,
Bombs away is your punishment.
Pulverize the Eiffel Towers,
Who criticize your government.
Bang, bang goes the broken glass and
*Kill all the f**s that don't agree.*
Trials by fire setting fire
Is not a way that's meant for me.

BOULEVARD OF BROKEN DREAMS

Words by Billie Joe
Music by Green Day
Arranged by Carol Matz

8
G D Am C
on the bou - le - vard of bro - ken dreams, where the cit - y sleeps and
what's f***ed up and ev - 'ry - thing's al - right. Check my vi - tal signs and
10
G D Am C
I'm the on - ly one and I walk a - lone.
know I'm still a - live and I walk a - lone.
12
G D Am C G D
I walk a - lone, I walk a - lone. I walk a - lone, I walk a...
Chorus:
15
F C G Am F C
My shad - ow's the on - ly one that walks be - side me. My shal - low heart's
f

18
G Am F C G Am
the on - ly thing that's beat-ing. Some-times I wish some-one out there will find me.
to Coda
21
F C E Am C
'Til then I walk a - lone. Ah. Ah.
ff
mf
24
G D Am C G D
Ah. Ah. Ah. Ah. Ah.
Verse 3:
27
Am C G D Am C
I walk this emp - ty street on the bou - le - vard of bro - ken dreams, where the cit - y sleeps and
mp

30
G
D
D.S. al Coda
Coda
E
I'm the on - ly one and I walk a...
a - lone.
33
A5
F
G5
D/F♯
C
A♭5
Cit - y of the dead.
Cit - y of the damned.
36
Cit - y of the damned.
Signs mis - lead - ing
39
to no - where.

ARE WE THE WAITING

11
D
F♯m
wait - ing un - known? This dirt - y town was
wait - ing un - known? The rage and love, the

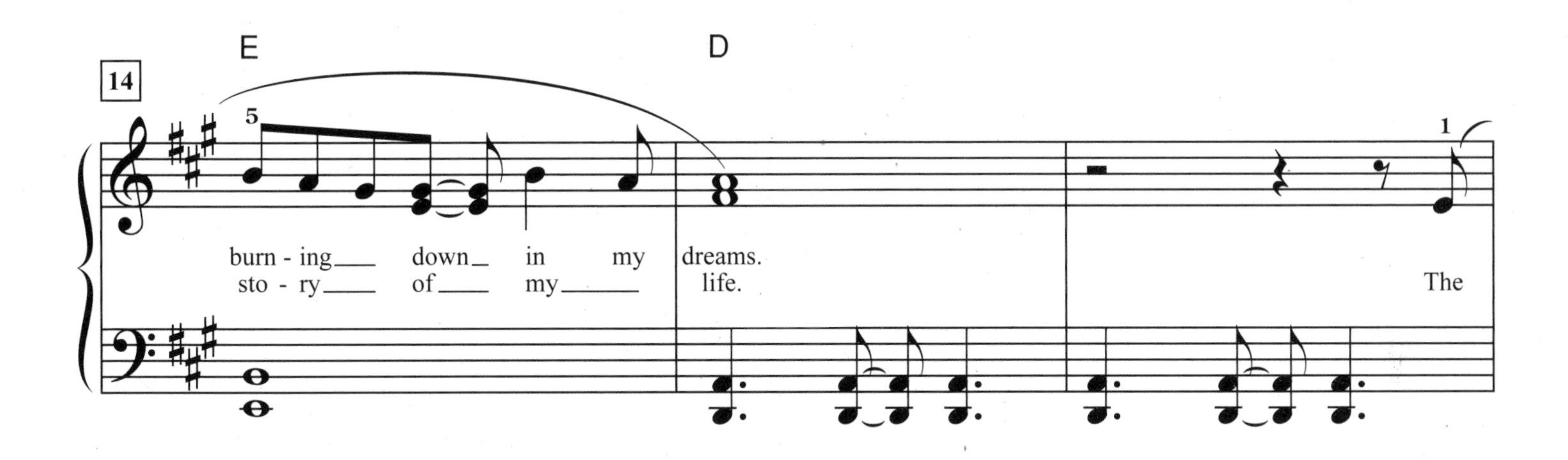
14
E
D
burn - ing down in my dreams.
sto - ry of my life. The

17
F♯m
E
D
Lost and found, cit - y bound in my dreams.
Je - sus of Sub - ur - bi - a is a lie.

20
Chorus:
A
And scream - ing...
Are we, we are,
are we, we are the

23
D
A
wait - ing? And scream - ing... Are we, we are,

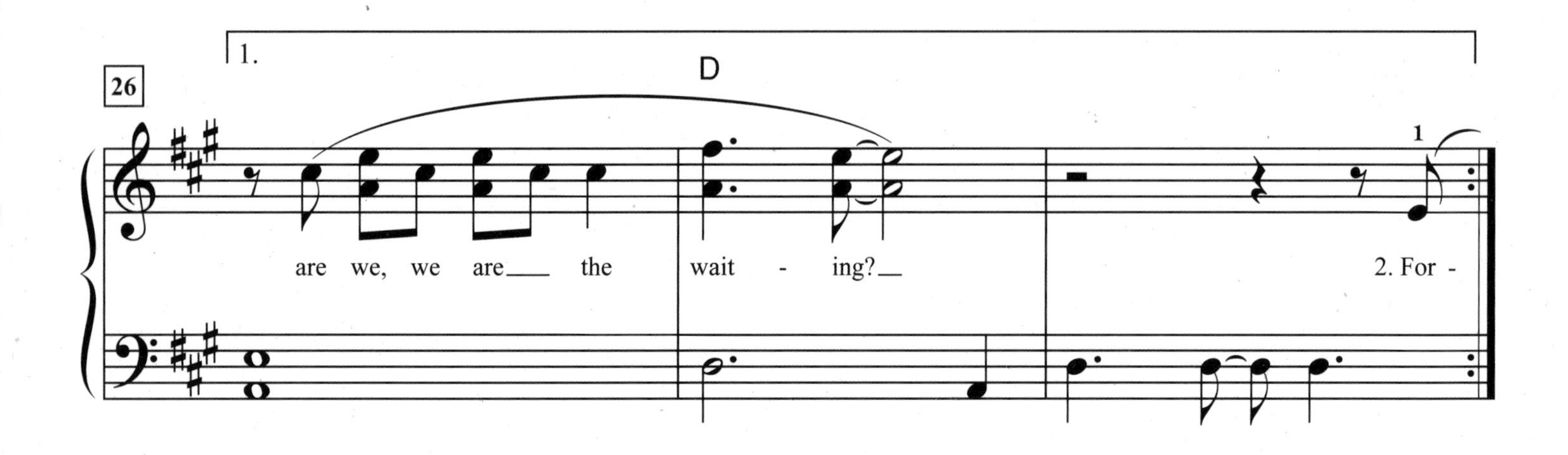
26
1.
D
are we, we are the wait - ing?
2. For -

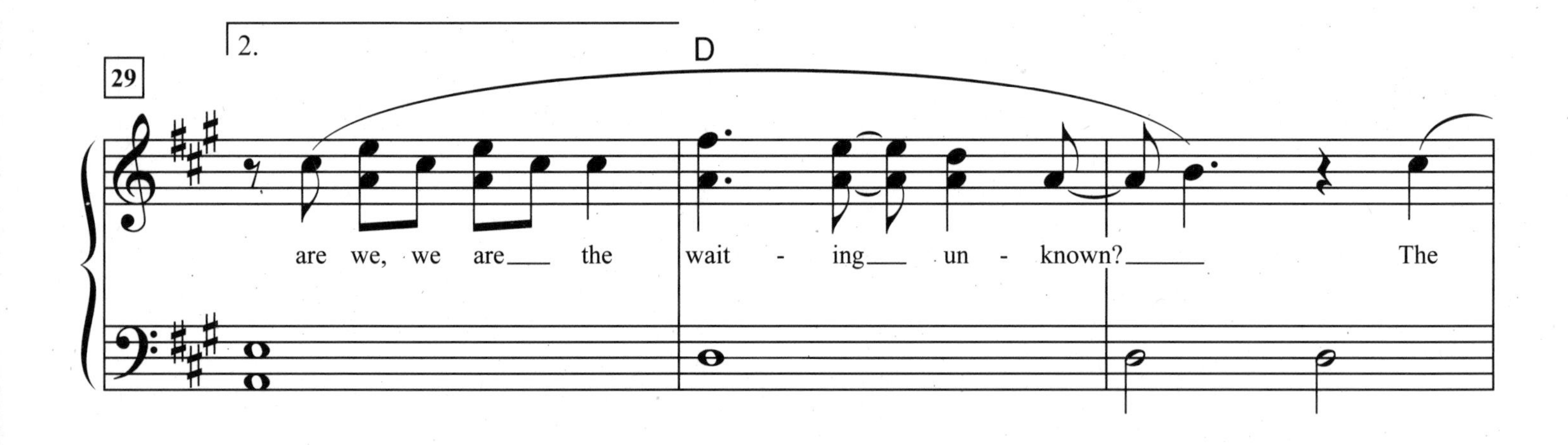
29
2.
D
are we, we are the wait - ing un - known? The

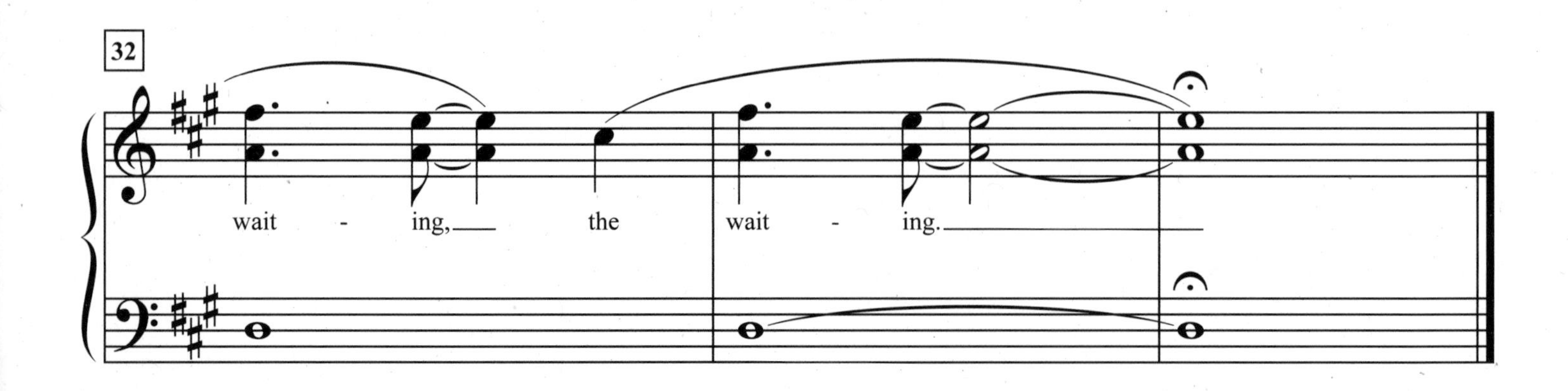
32
wait - ing, the wait - ing.

LAST OF THE AMERICAN GIRLS/ SHE'S A REBEL

Words by Billie Joe
Music by Green Day
Arranged by Carol Matz

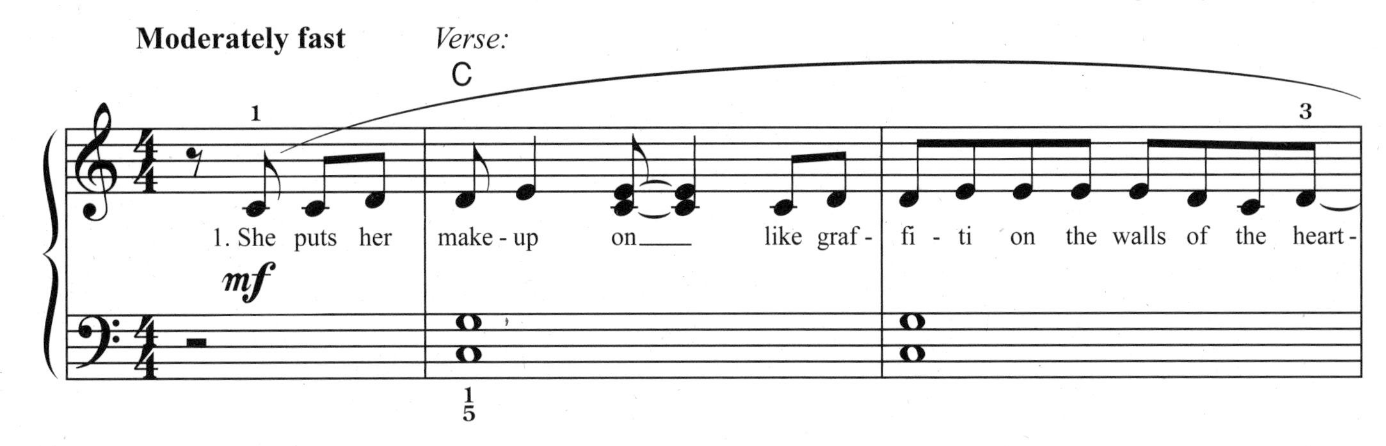

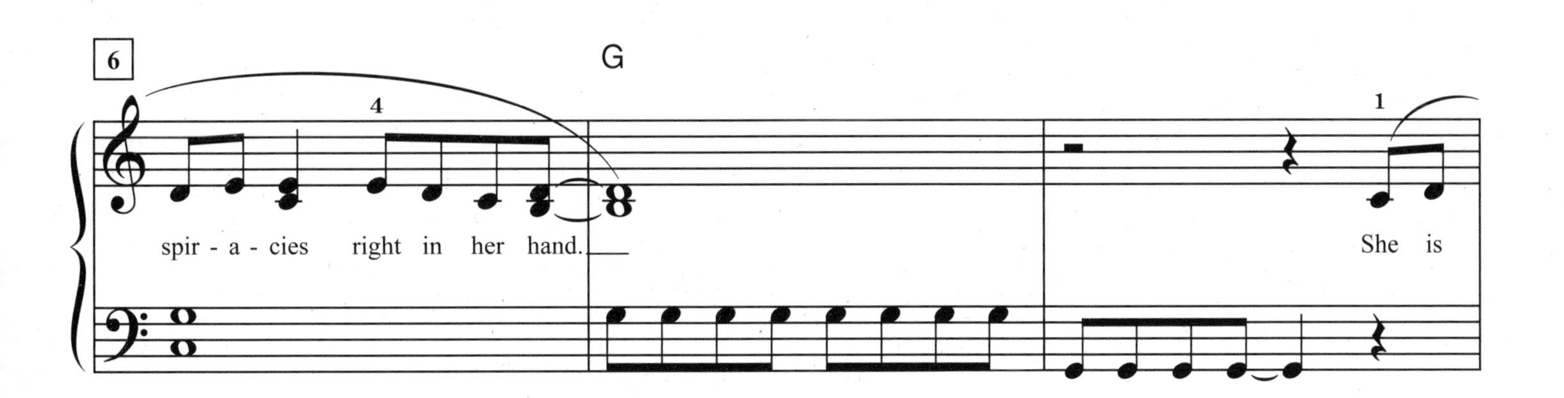

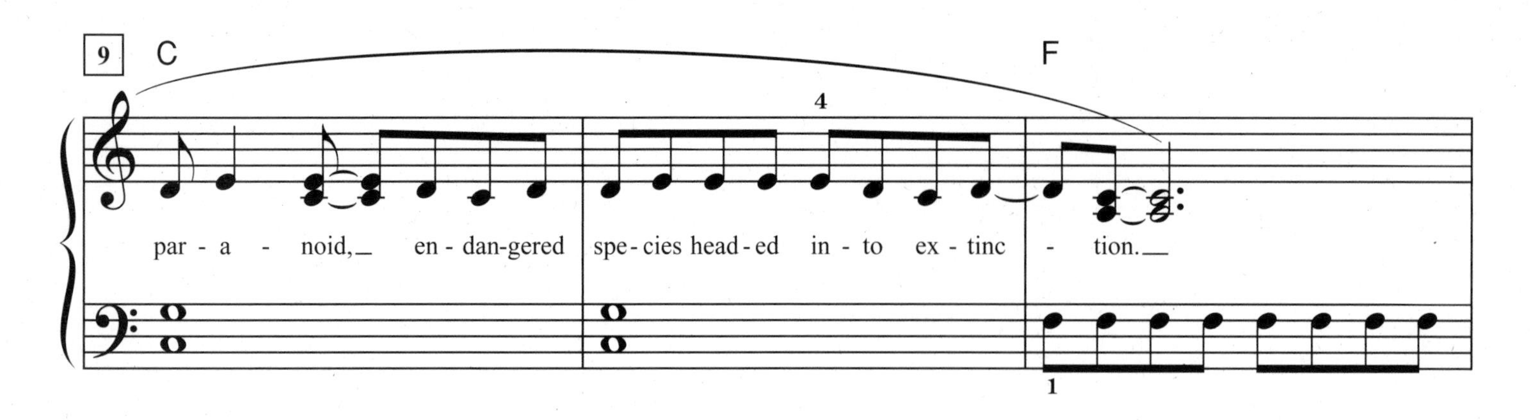
9
C
F
par - a - noid, en - dan-gered spe - cies head - ed in - to ex - tinc - tion.

12
C
G N.C.
She is one of a kind. Well, she's the last of the A - mer - i - can

15
C
girls. (She's a reb - el, she's a saint.) 2. She wears her o - ver - coat for the

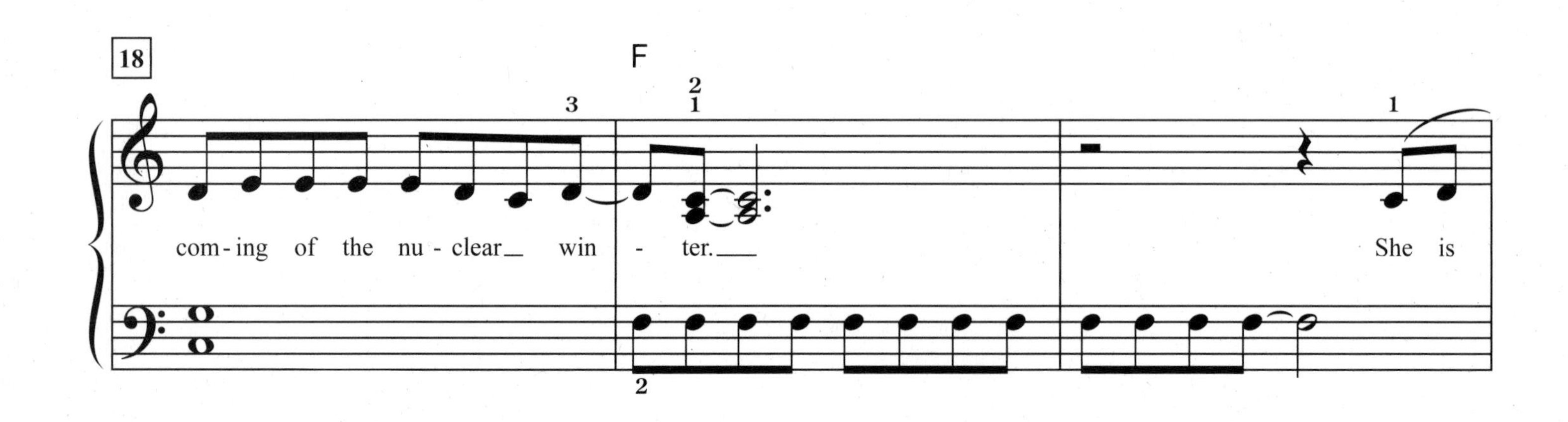
18
F
com - ing of the nu - clear win - ter. She is

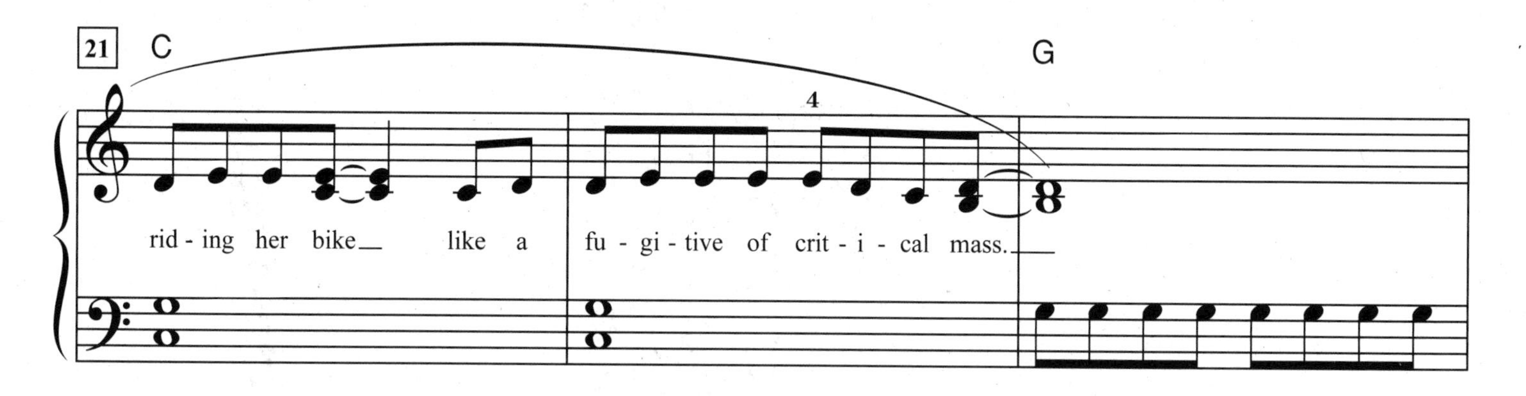
21
C
G
4
rid - ing her bike like a fu - gi - tive of crit - i - cal mass.

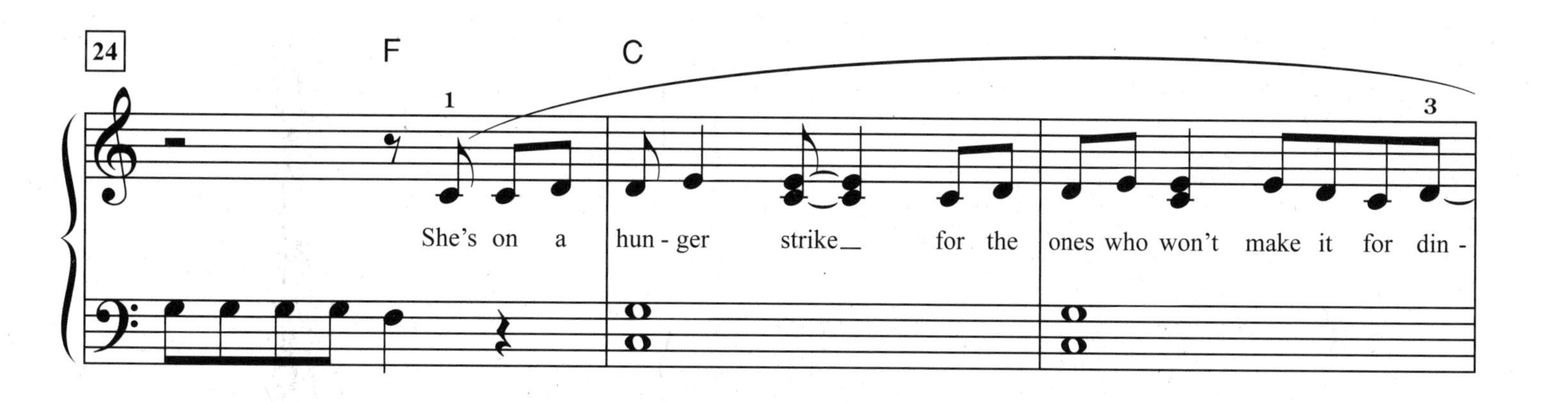
24
F
C
1
3
She's on a hun - ger strike for the ones who won't make it for din -

27
F
C
1
- ner.
She makes e - nough to sur - vive for a

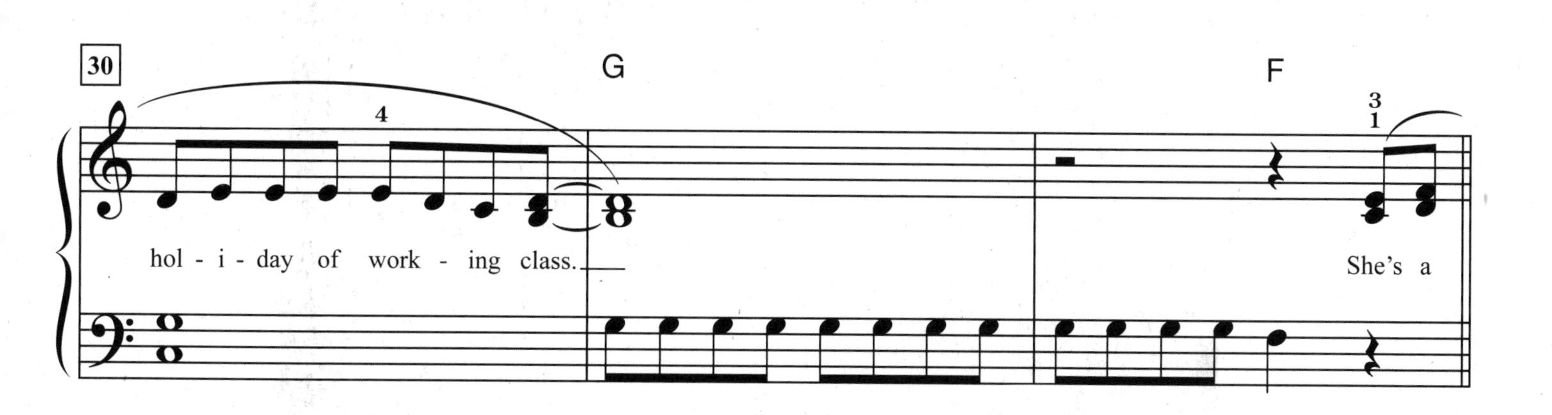
30
G
F
4
3
1
hol - i - day of work - ing class.
She's a

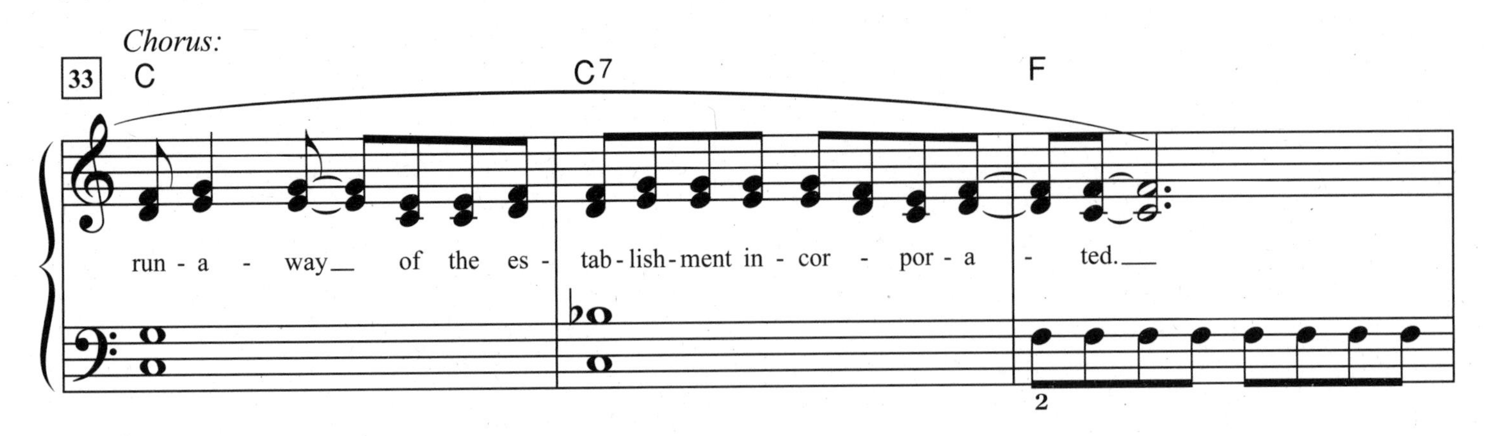
Chorus:
33
C
C7
F
run - a - way__ of the es - tab - lish - ment in - cor - por - a - ted.__
2

36
Fm
C
G
N.C.
She won't co - op - er - ate.__ Well, she's the last of the A - mer - i - can
1
2

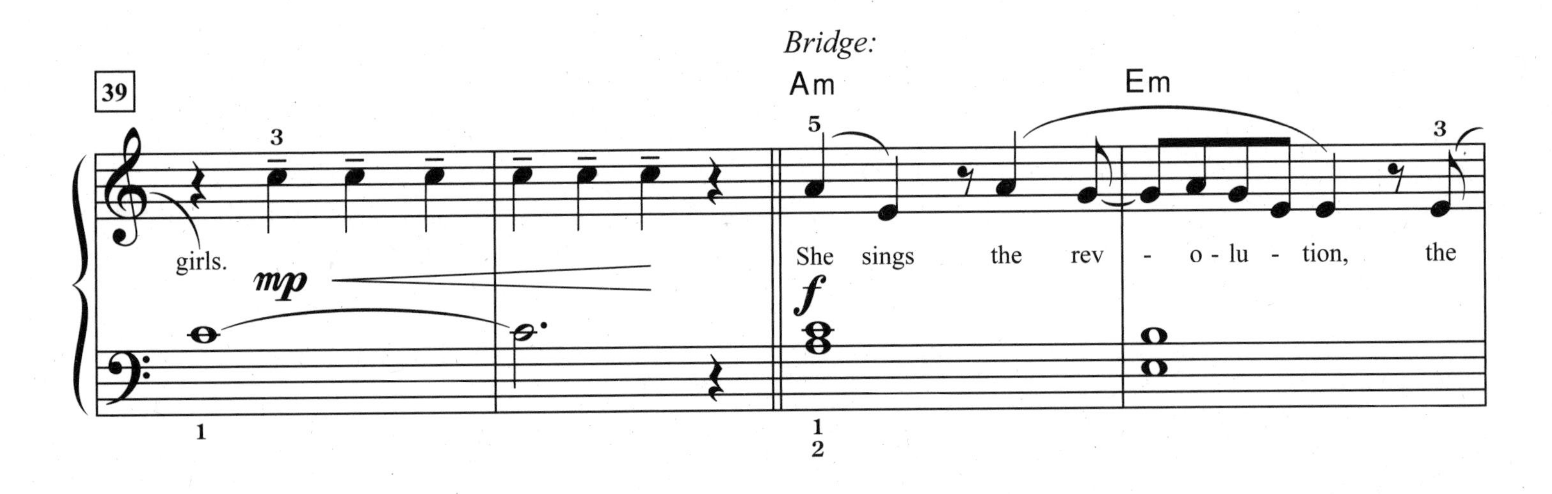
39
Bridge:
Am
Em
3
5
3
girls.
mp
She sings the rev - o - lu - tion, the
f
1
1
2

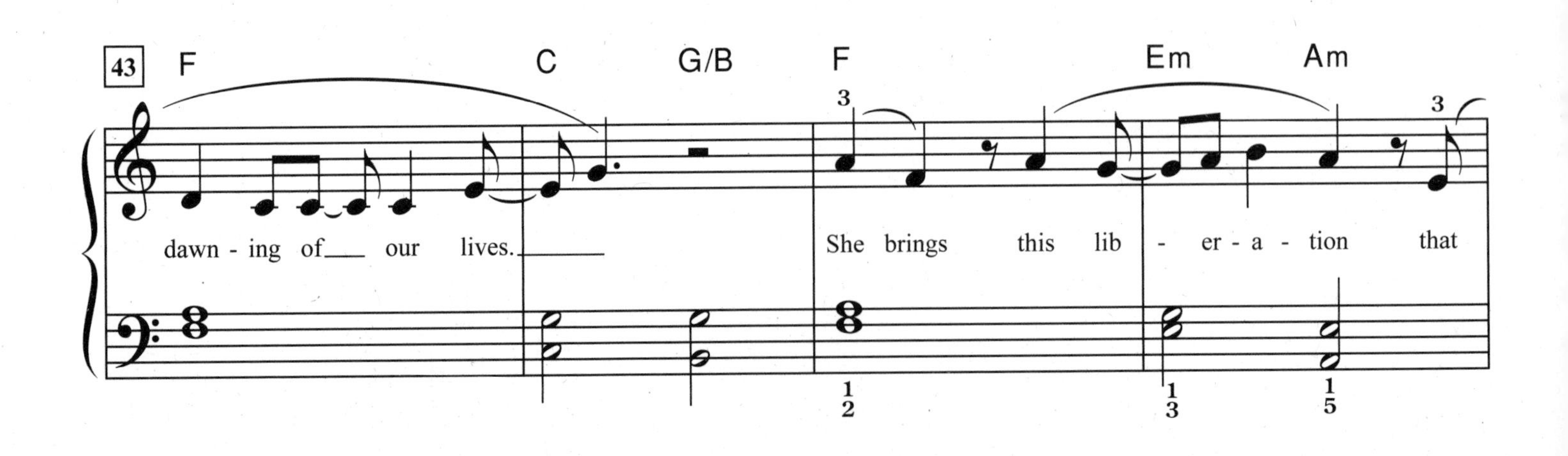
43
F
C
G/B
F
Em
Am
3
3
dawn - ing of__ our lives.______
She brings this lib - er - a - tion that
1
2
1
3
1
5

47
B♭
G
N.C.
I just can't de - fine.
Well, noth - ing comes to
mind.
Yeah!

50
C
She's a reb - el,
she's a saint,
she's the salt of the
She's a reb - el,
vig - i - lan - te,
miss - ing link on the

53
G
F
D
G
D
G
earth and she's dan - ger - ous.
brink of de - struc - tion.
She's a reb - el.
She's a reb - el.

56
D
G
A
G
D
She's a reb - el,
and she's dan - ger - ous.

LAST NIGHT ON EARTH

Lyrics by Billie Joe
Music by Green Day
Arranged by Carol Matz

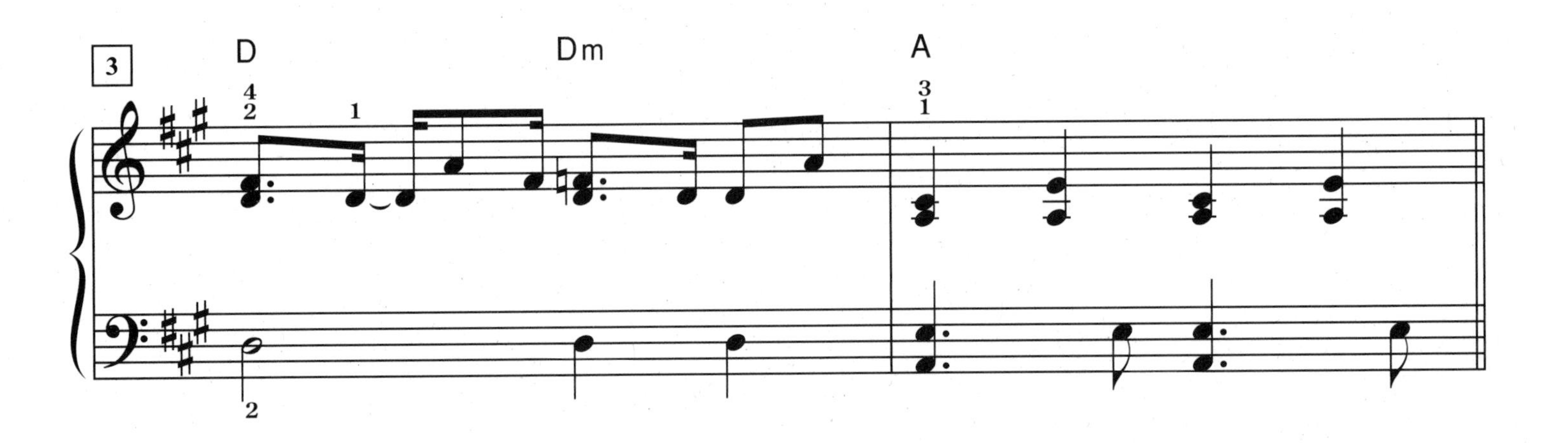

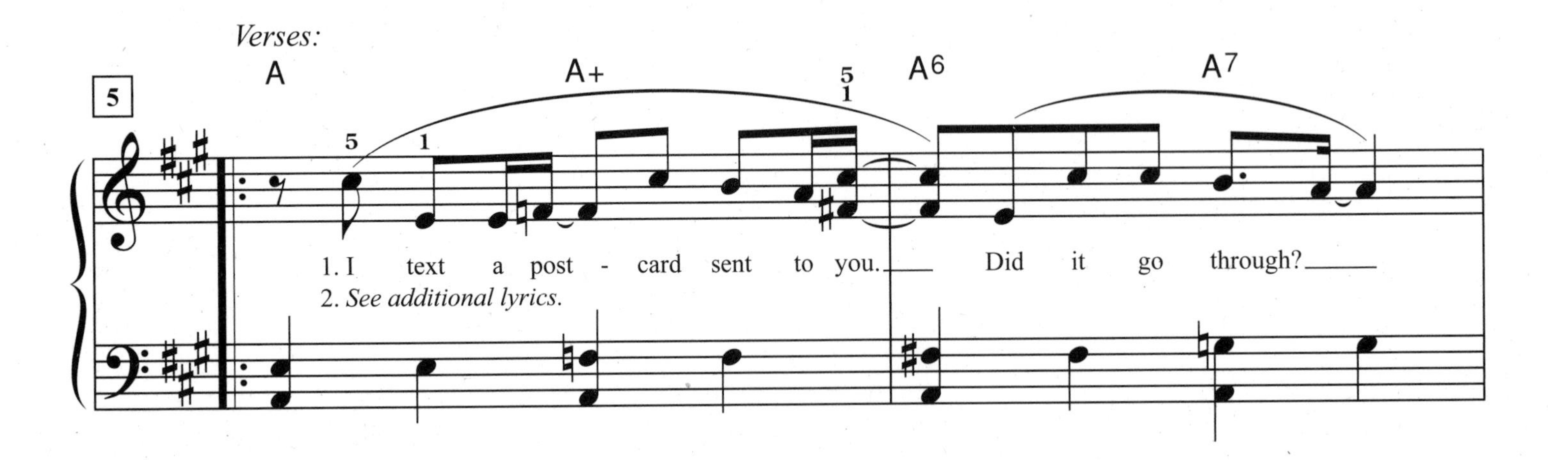

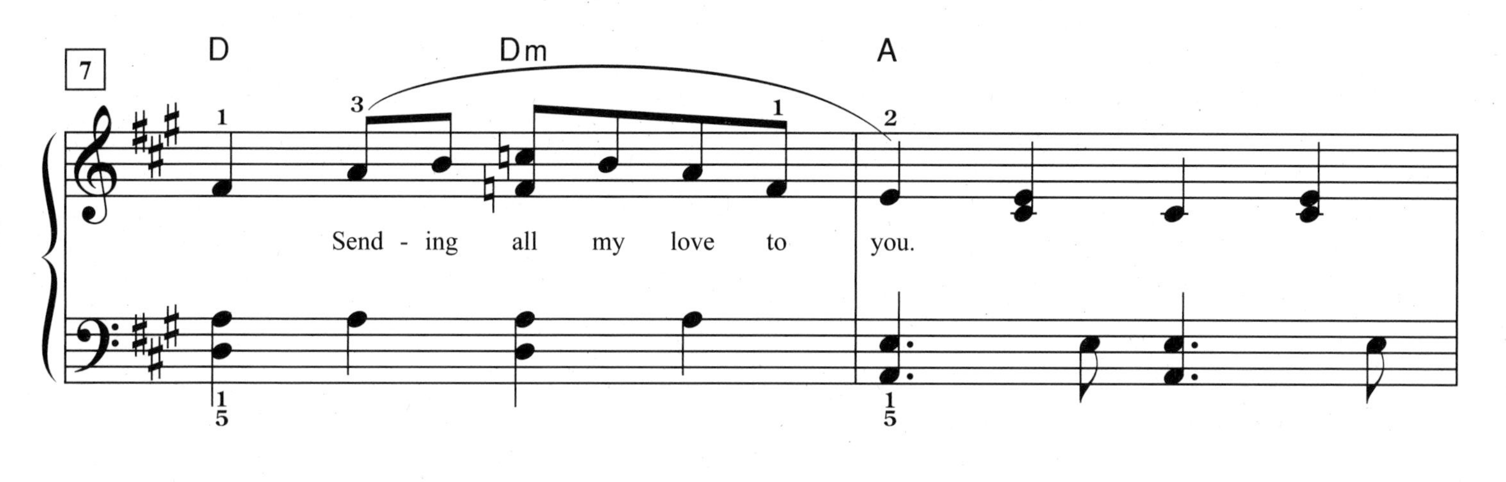
7
D
Dm
A
Send - ing all my love to you.

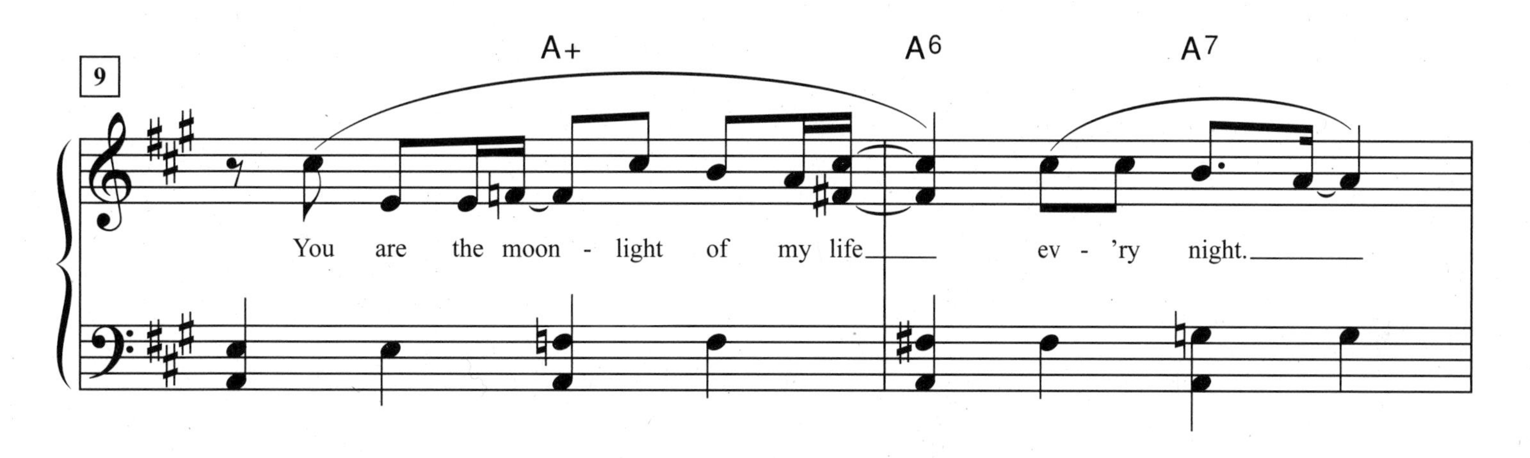
9
A+
A6
A7
You are the moon - light of my life ev - 'ry night.

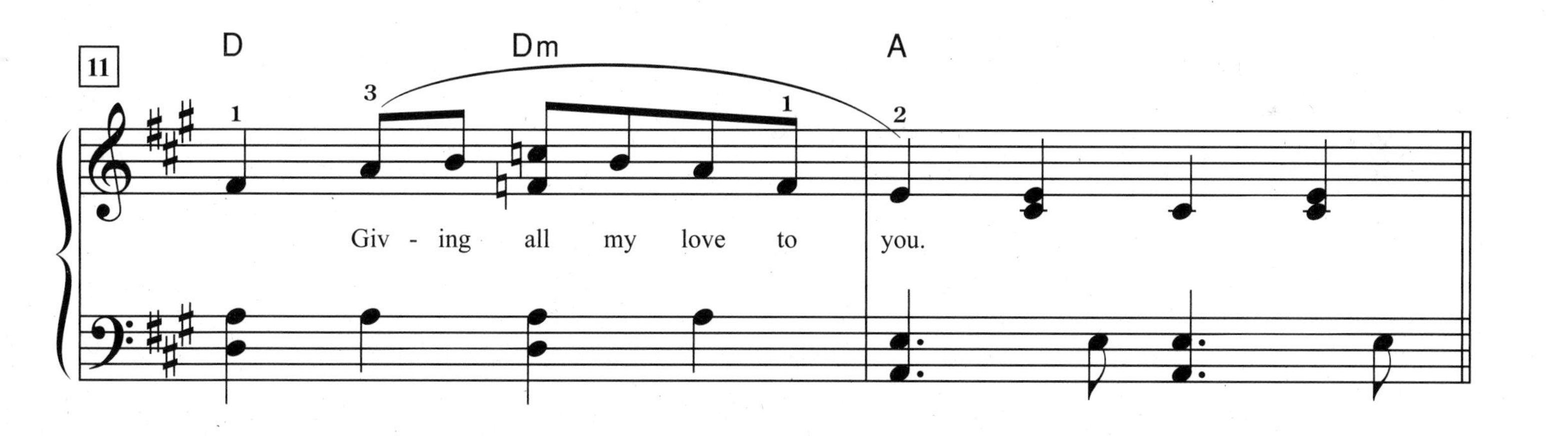
11
D
Dm
A
Giv - ing all my love to you.

Chorus:
13
D
Dm
A
My beat - ing heart be - longs to you.

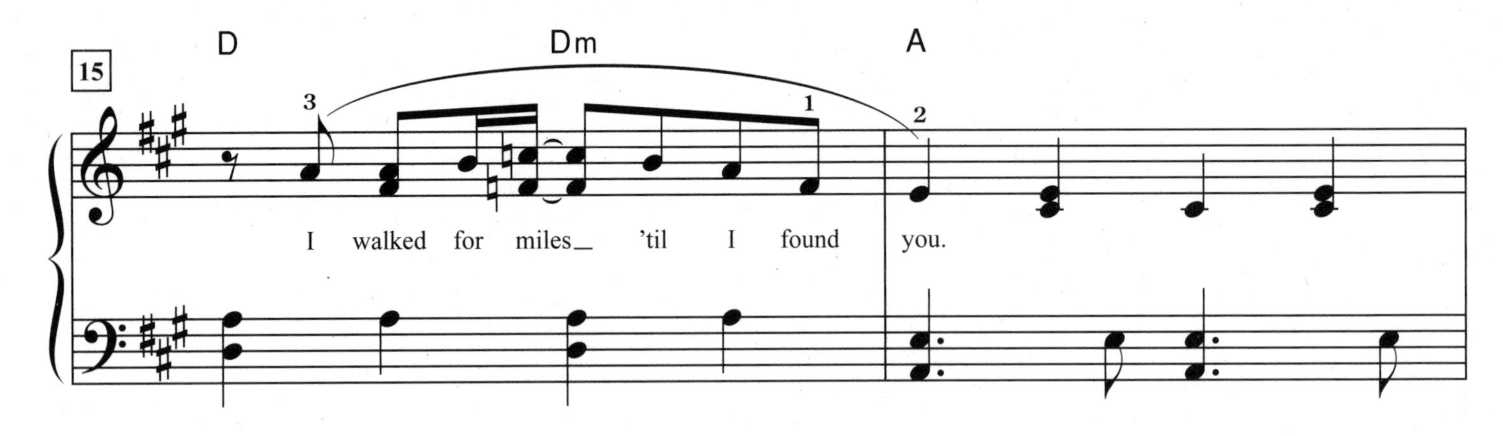
15
D
Dm
A
I walked for miles_ 'til I found you.

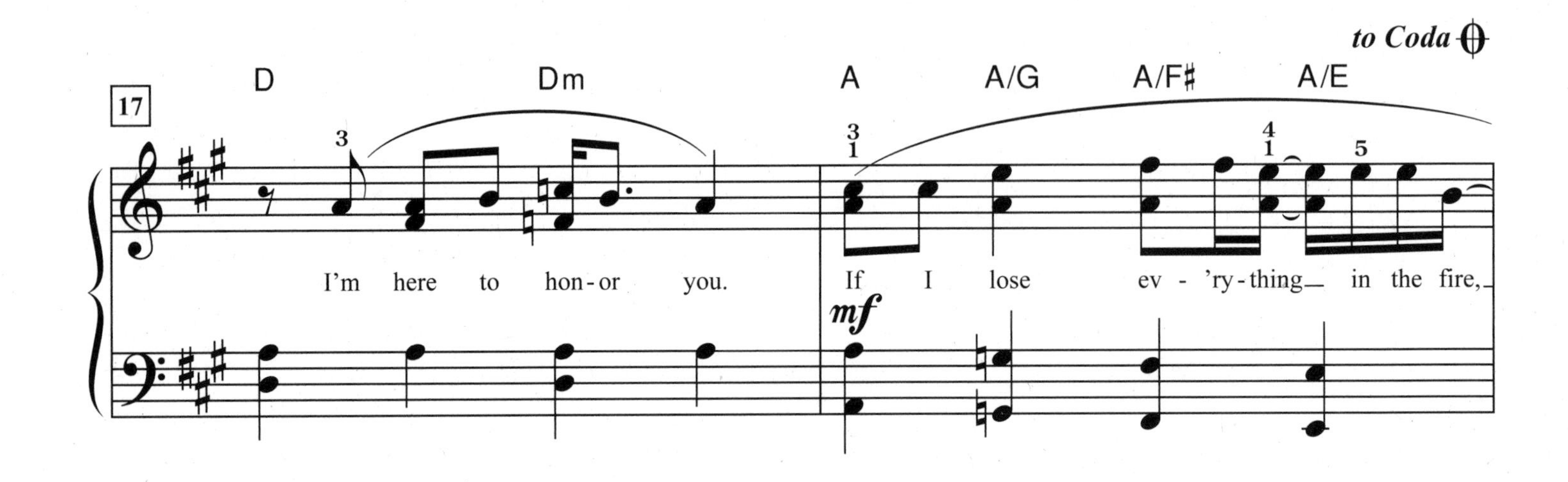
to Coda
17
D
Dm
A
A/G
A/F♯
A/E
I'm here to hon-or you.
If I lose ev - 'ry-thing_ in the fire,_
mf

19
D
Dm
A
A+
I'm send-ing all my love to you._
mp

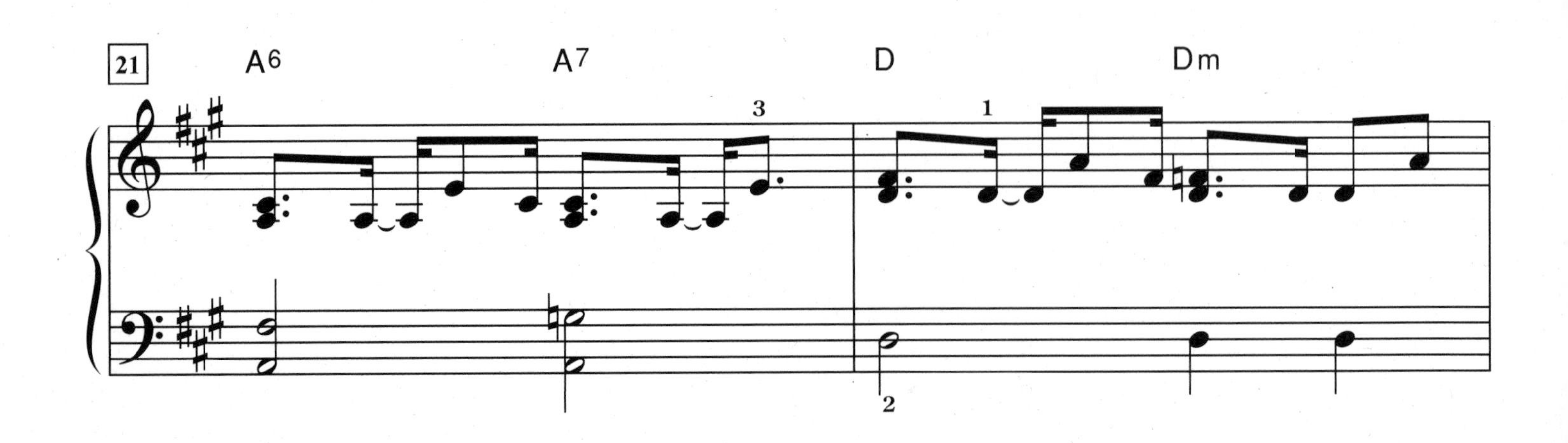
21
A6
A7
D
Dm

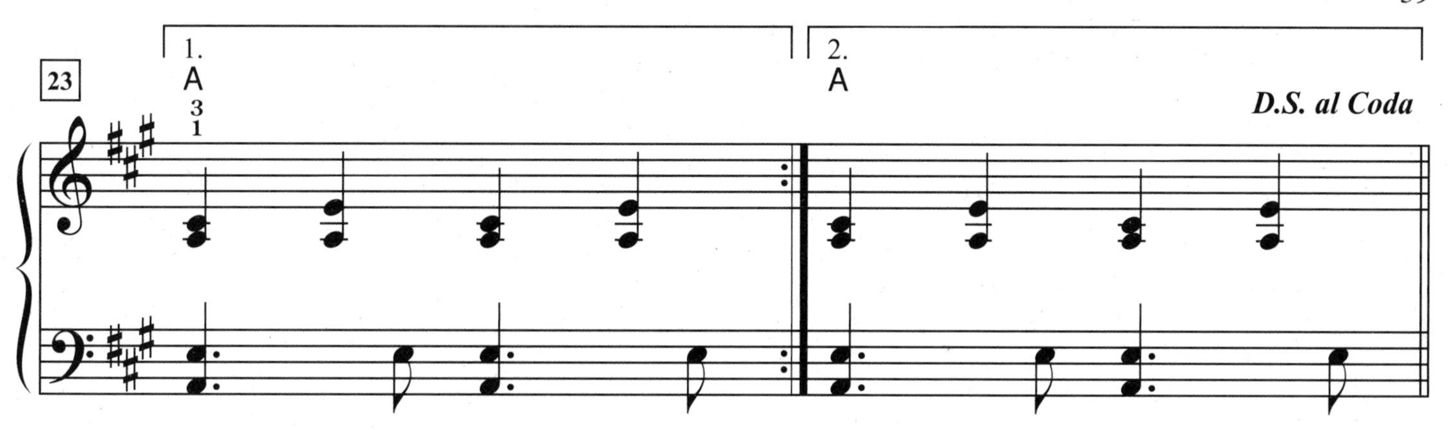

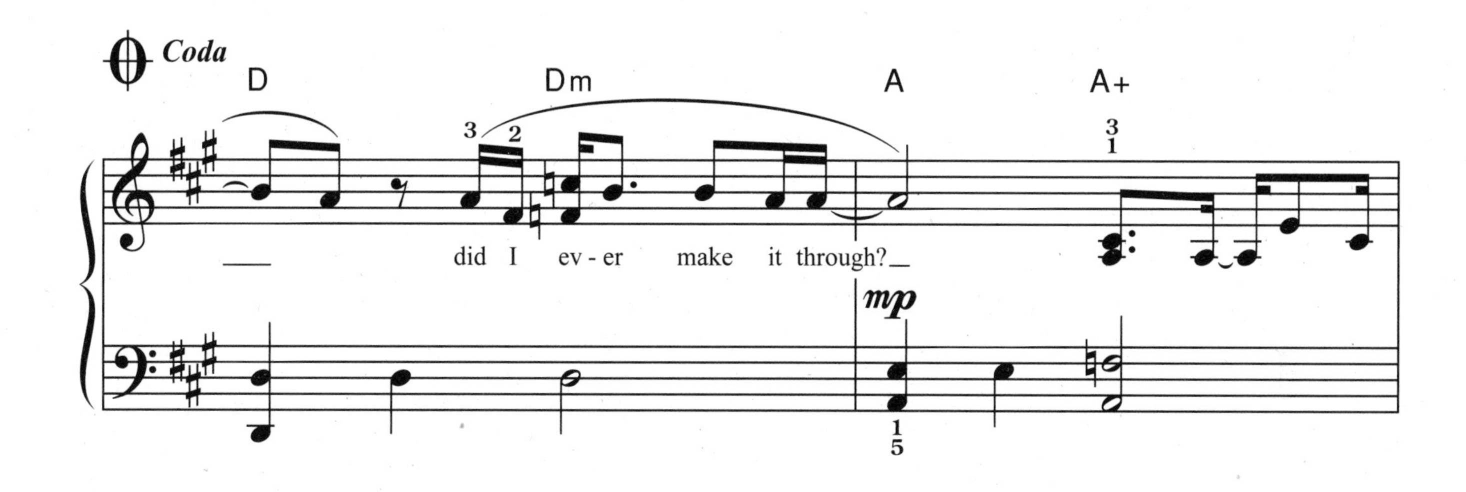

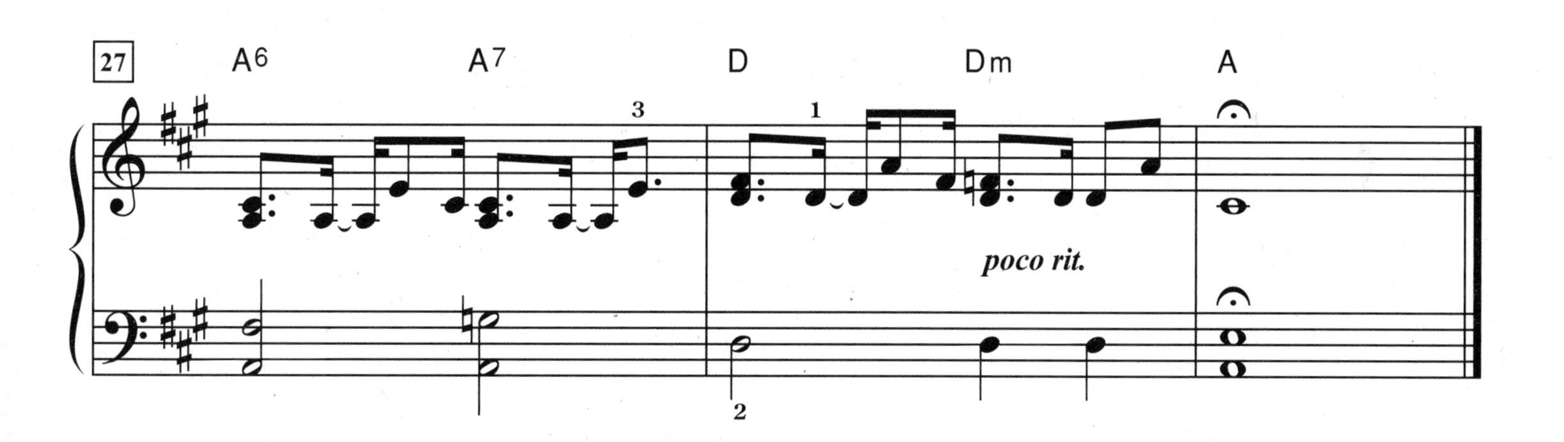

Verse 2:
With every breath that I am worth here on earth,
I'm sending all my love to you.
So if you dare to second guess
You can rest assured that all my love's for you.

BEFORE THE LOBOTOMY

Lyrics by Billie Joe
Music by Green Day
Arranged by Carol Matz

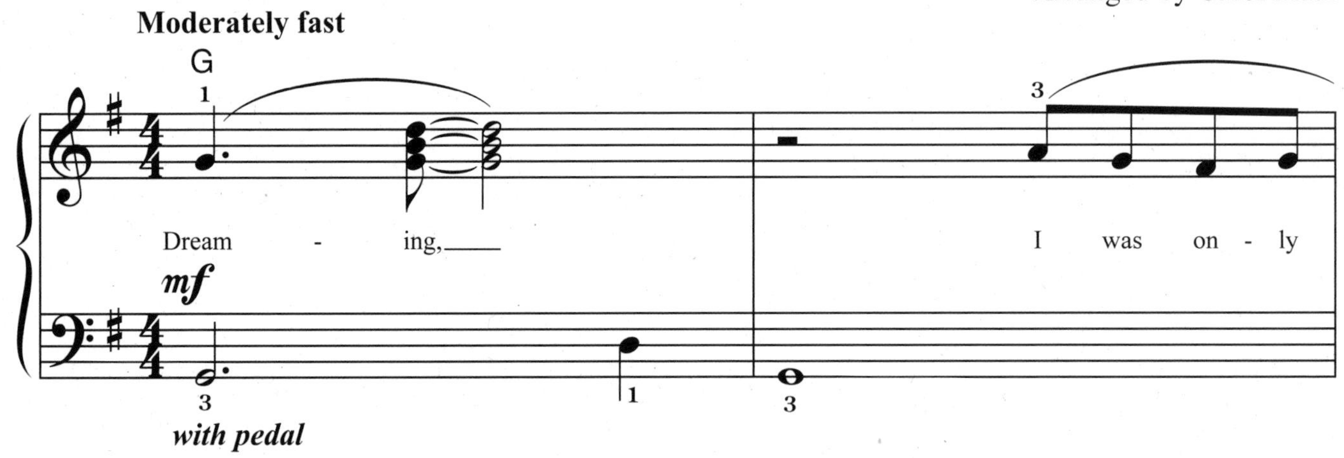

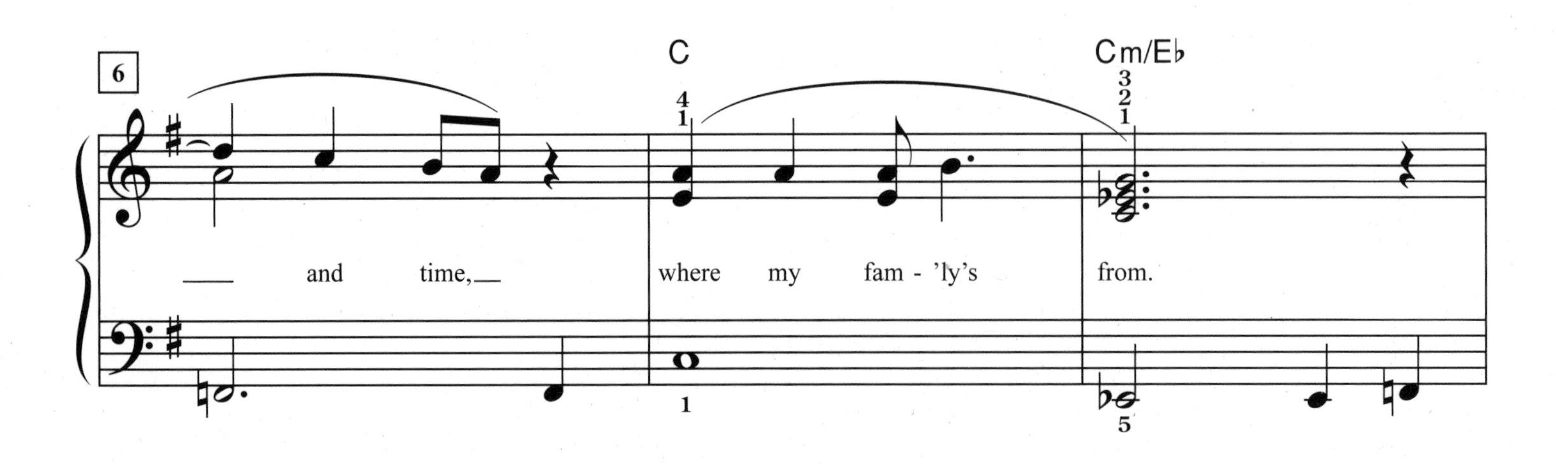

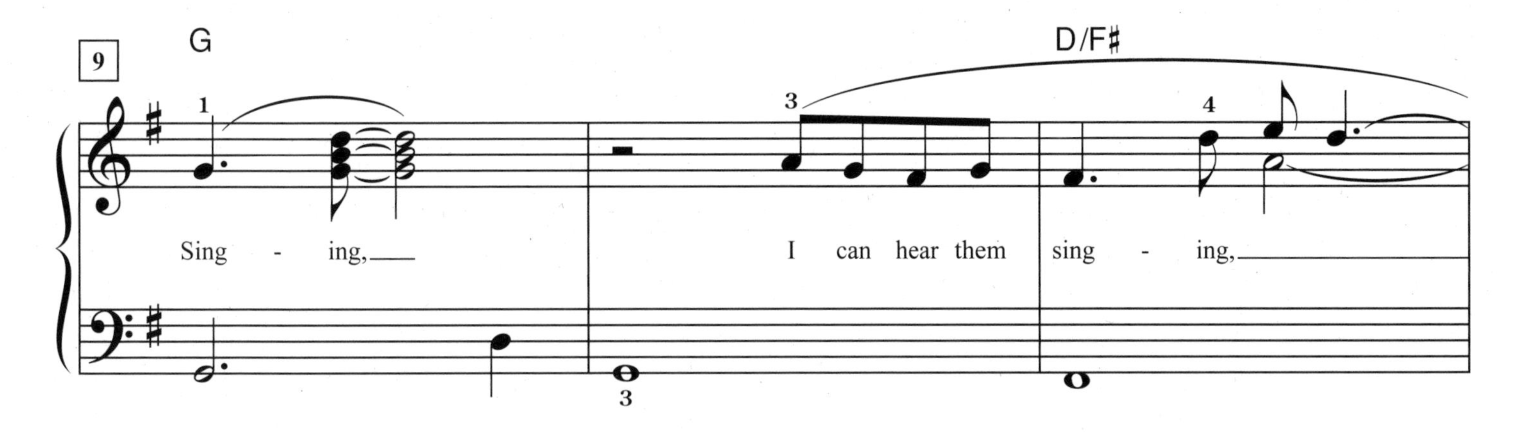
9
G
D/F♯
Sing - ing,
I can hear them sing - ing,

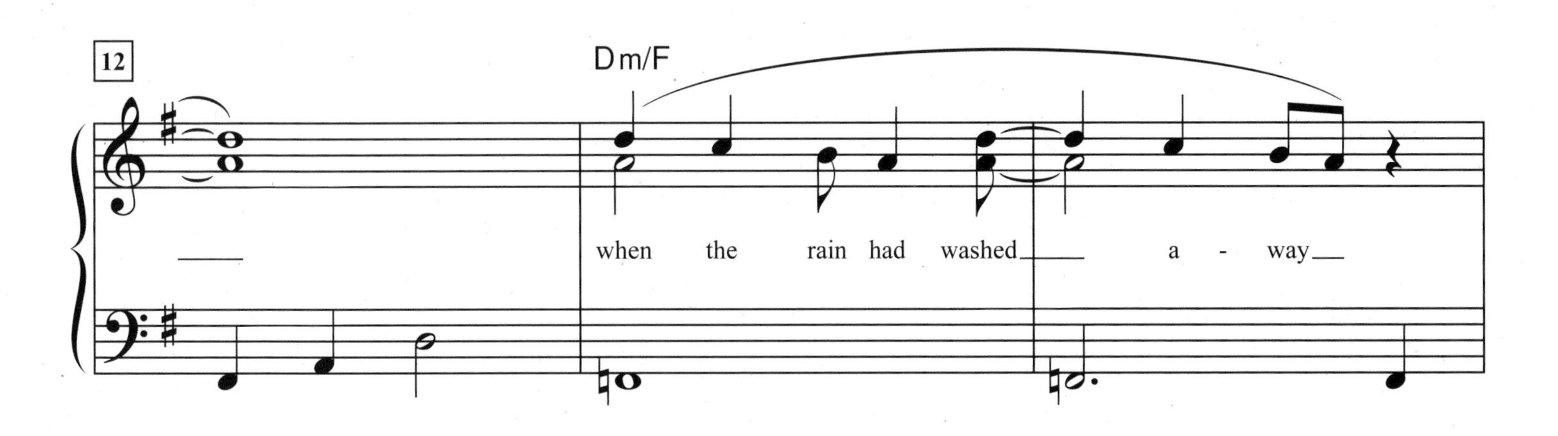
12
Dm/F
when the rain had washed a - way

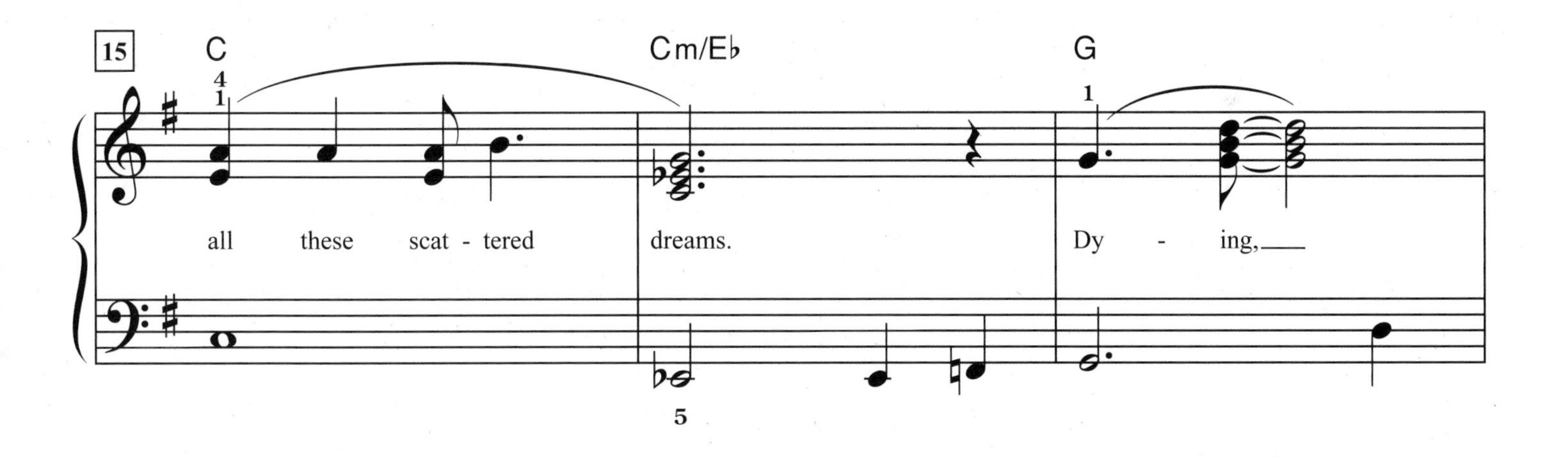
15
C
Cm/E♭
G
all these scat - tered dreams.
Dy - ing,

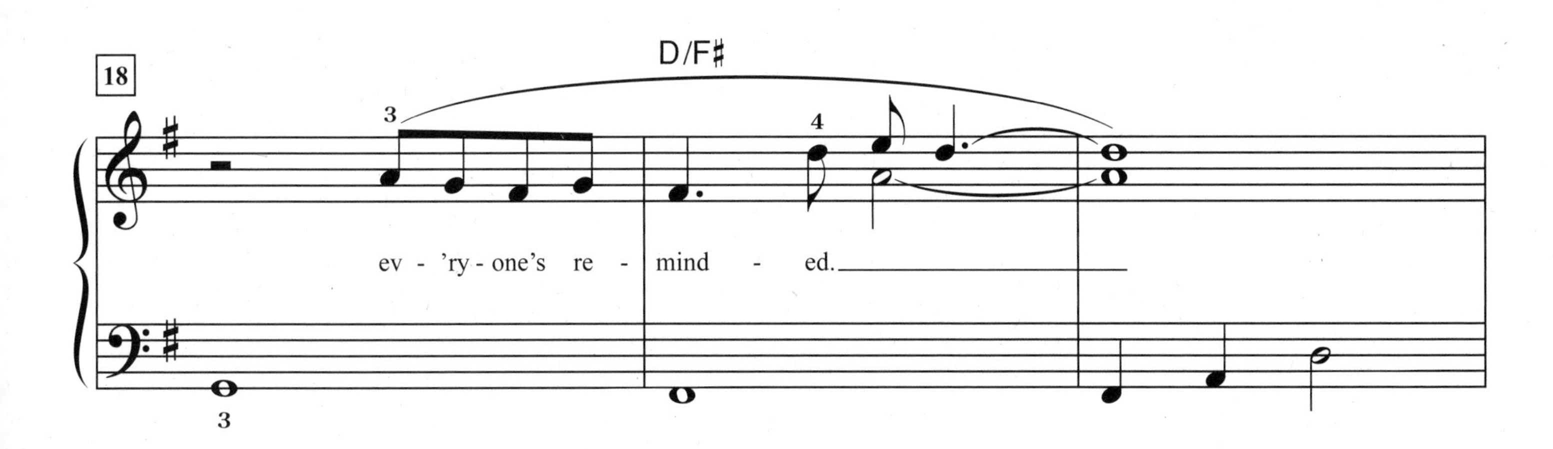
18
D/F♯
ev - 'ry - one's re - mind - ed.

21
Dm/F
C
Hearts are washed in mis - er - y,
drenched in gas - o -

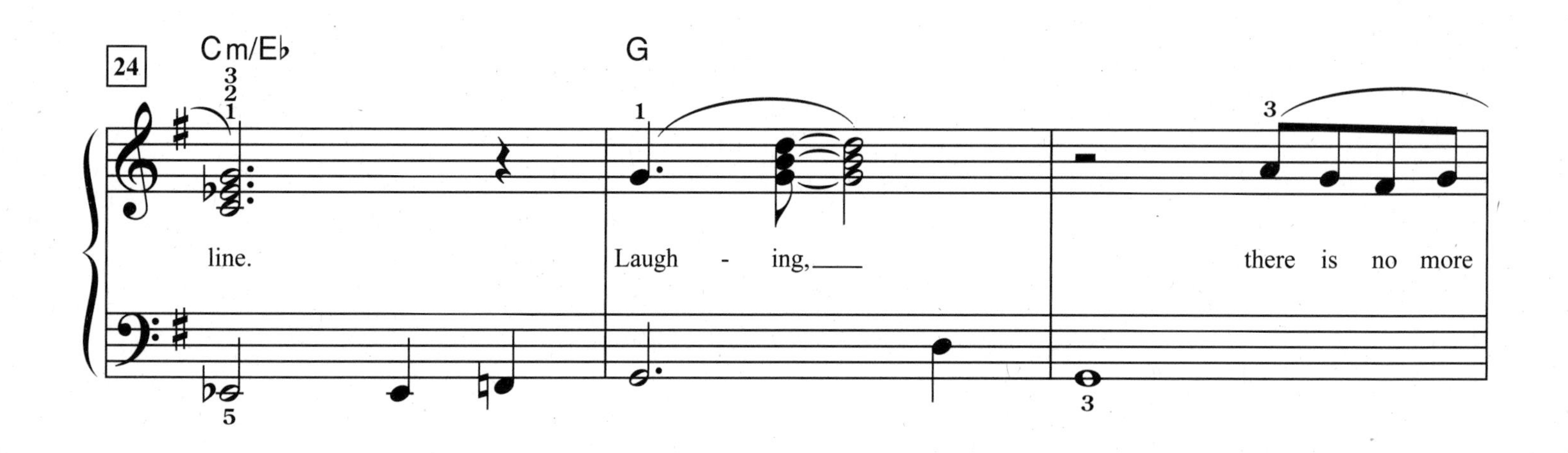
24
Cm/E♭
G
line.
Laugh - ing,
there is no more

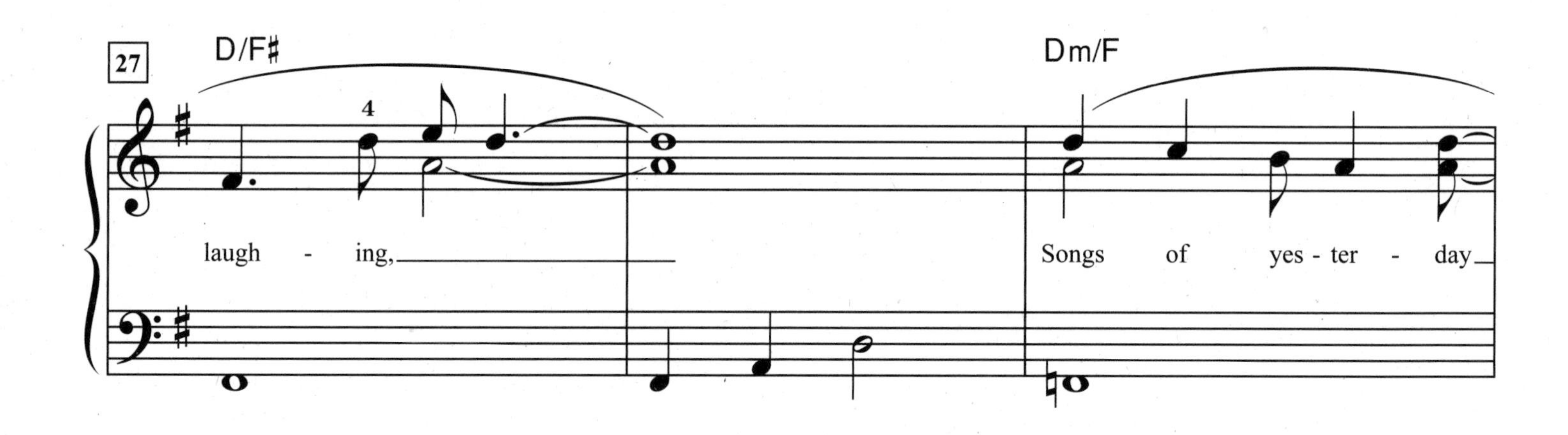
27
D/F♯
Dm/F
laugh - ing,
Songs of yes - ter - day

30
C
Cm/E♭
now live
in the un - der - ground.

WHEN IT'S TIME

Words and Music by Billie Joe
Arranged by Carol Matz

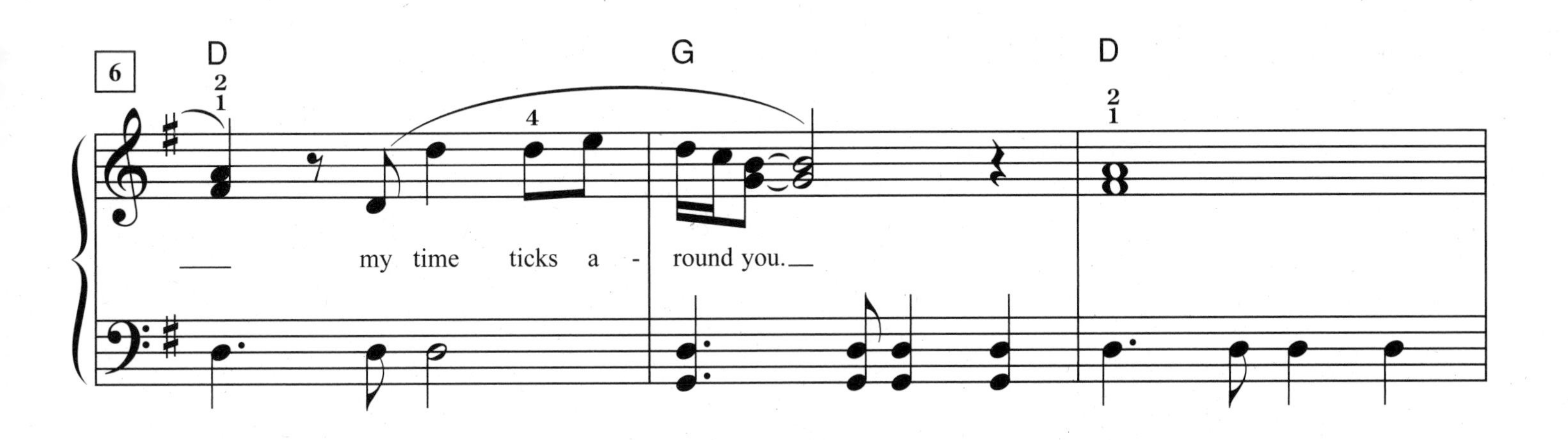

9
G
D/F♯
4
But then I need your voice as the key to

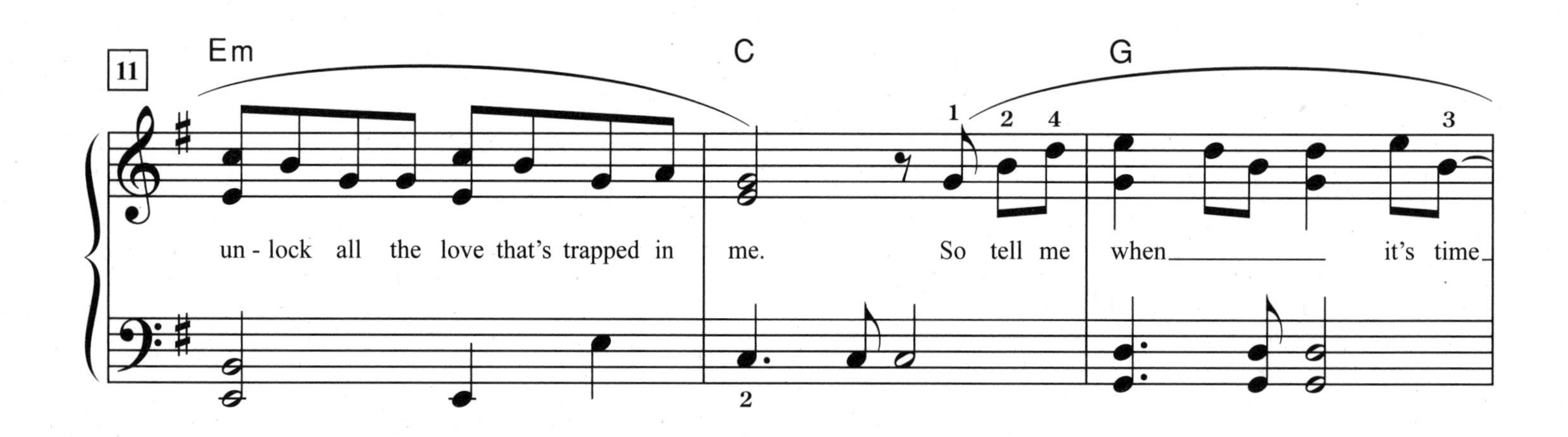
11
Em
C
G
1 2 4
3
2
un - lock all the love that's trapped in me. So tell me when it's time

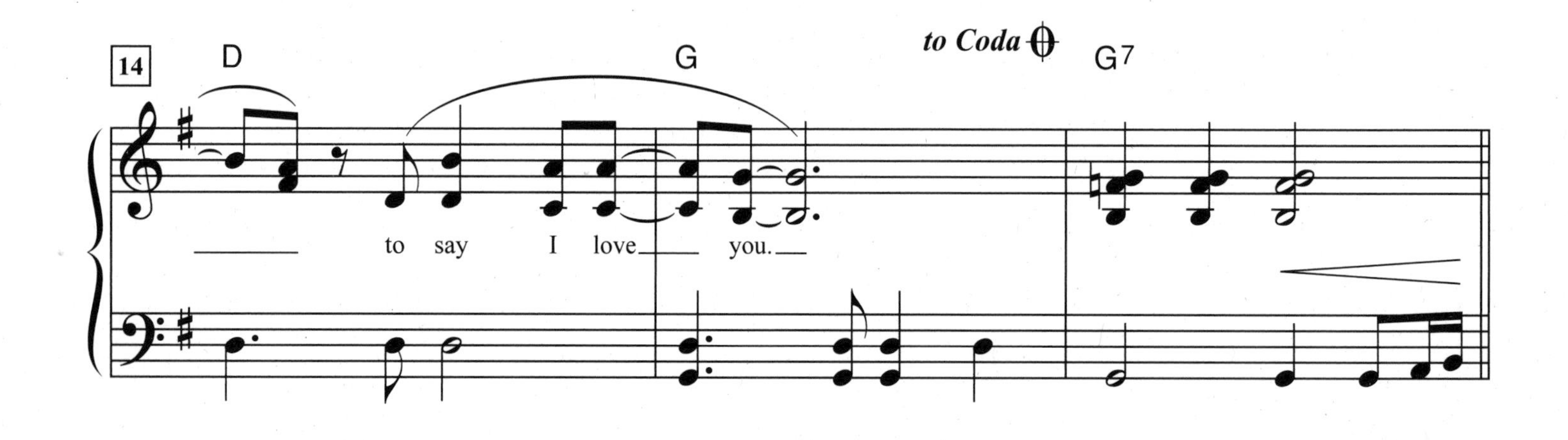
14
D
G
to Coda
G7
to say I love you.

Chorus:
17
C
G
D
5
2
1 1
mf
All I want is you to un-der-stand that when I take your hand, it's 'cause I

Verse 2:
I feel lonely for
All the losers that will never take the time to say
What's really on their mind,
Instead they just hide away.
Yet they'll never have
Someone like you to guide them and help along the way,
Or tell them when it's time to say I love you.

KNOW YOUR ENEMY

Lyrics by Billie Joe
Music by Green Day
Arranged by Carol Matz

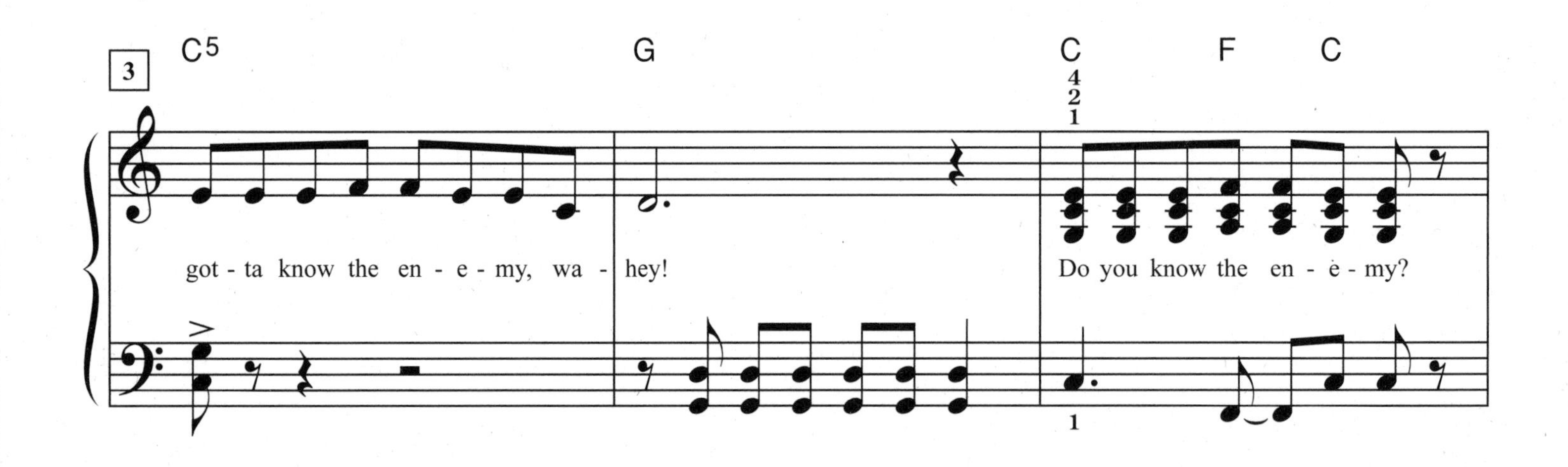

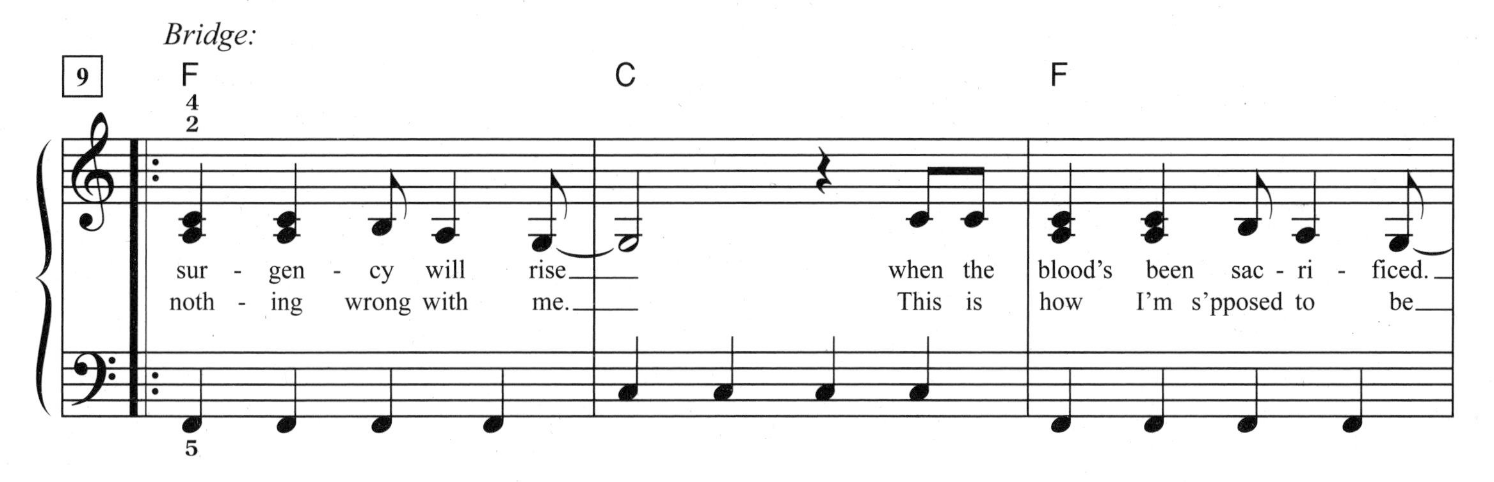
Bridge:
9
F C F
sur - gen - cy will rise when the blood's been sac - ri - ficed.
noth - ing wrong with me. This is how I'm s'pposed to be

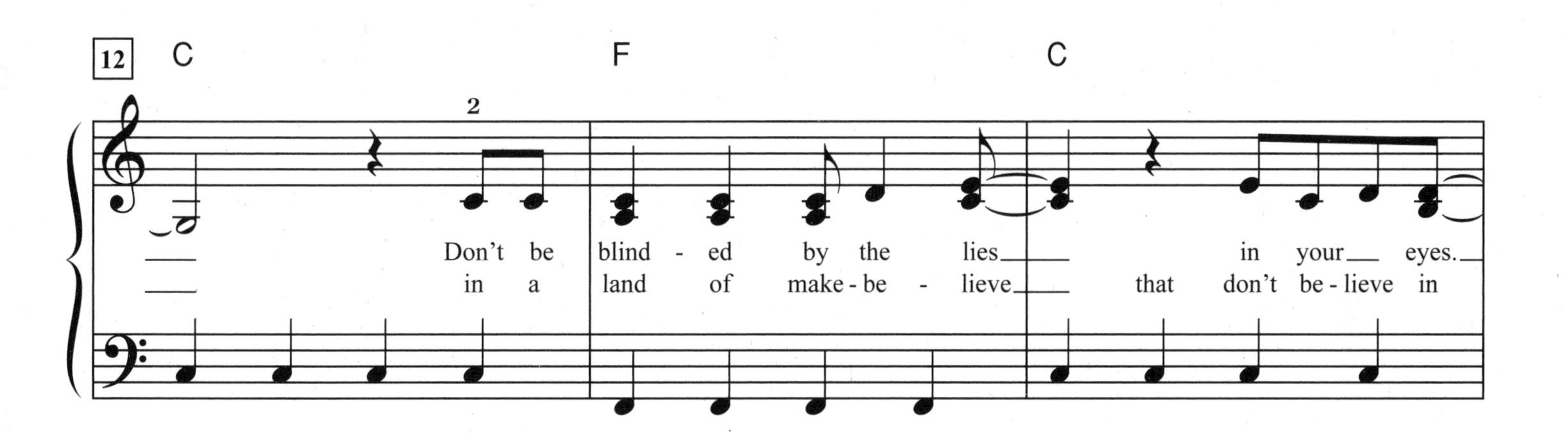
12
C F C
Don't be blind - ed by the lies in your eyes.
in a land of make - be - lieve that don't be - lieve in

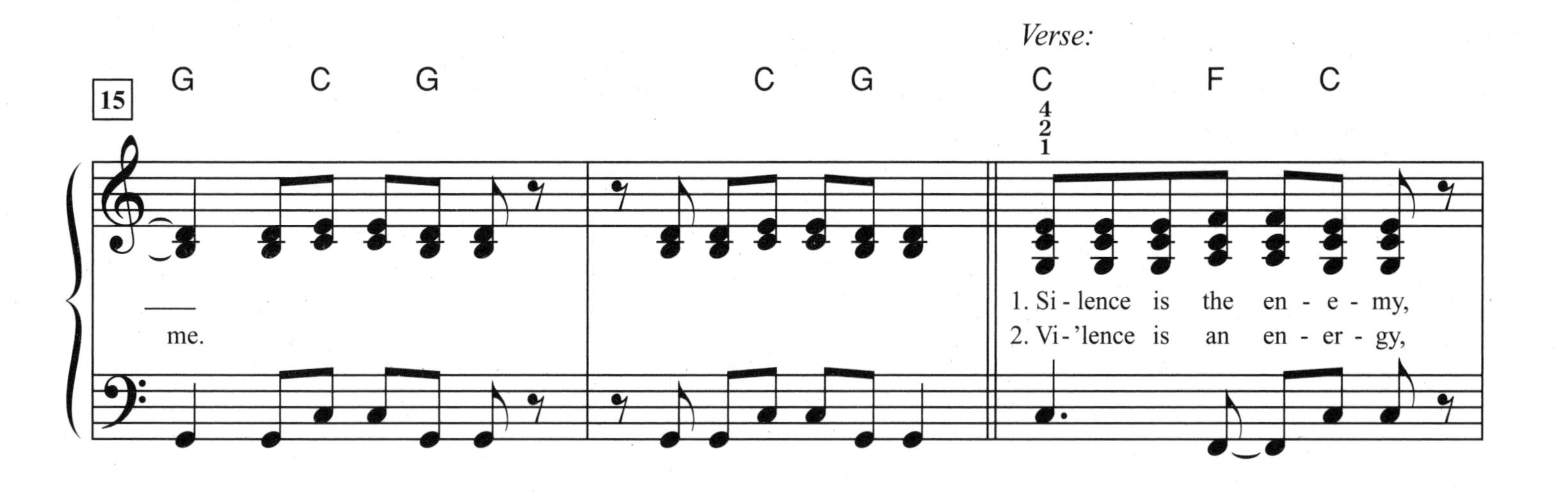
Verse:
15
G C G C G C F C
me.
1. Si - lence is the en - e - my,
2. Vi - 'lence is an en - er - gy,

18
F C B♭ C F C G
a - gainst your ur - gen - cy, so ral - ly up the de - mons of your soul.
a - gainst the en - e - my, well, vi - 'lence is an en - er - gy, wa - hey!

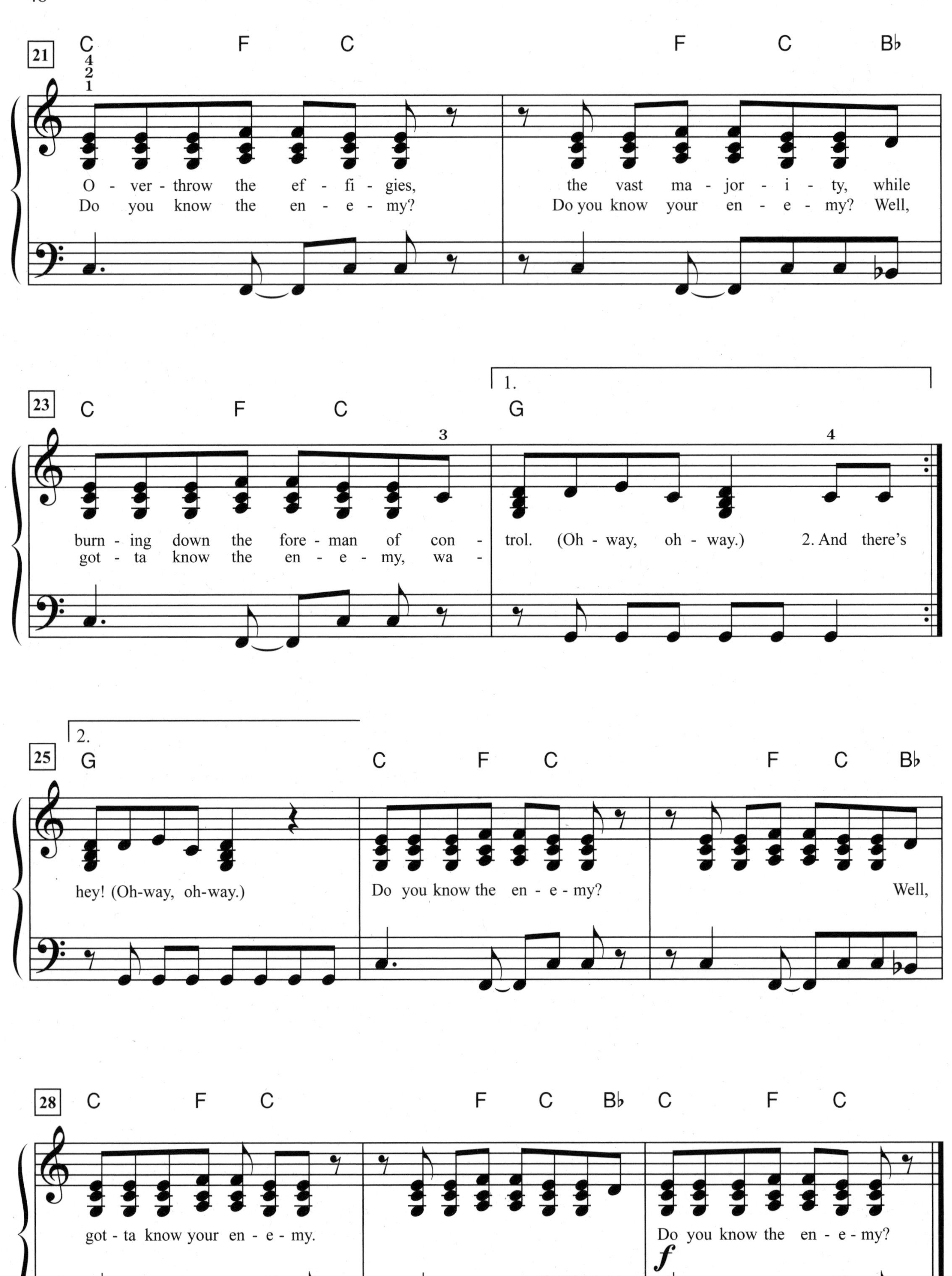
21
C
F
C
F
C
B♭
4
2
1
O - ver - throw the ef - fi - gies,
Do you know the en - e - my?
the vast ma - jor - i - ty, while
Do you know your en - e - my? Well,
23
C
F
C
3
1.
G
4
burn - ing down the fore - man of con -
got - ta know the en - e - my, wa -
trol. (Oh - way, oh - way.) 2. And there's
2.
25
G
C
F
C
F
C
B♭
hey! (Oh-way, oh-way.)
Do you know the en - e - my?
Well,
28
C
F
C
F
C
B♭
C
F
C
got - ta know your en - e - my.
Do you know the en - e - my?
f

21 GUNS

Lyrics by Billie Joe
Music by Green Day
Arranged by Carol Matz

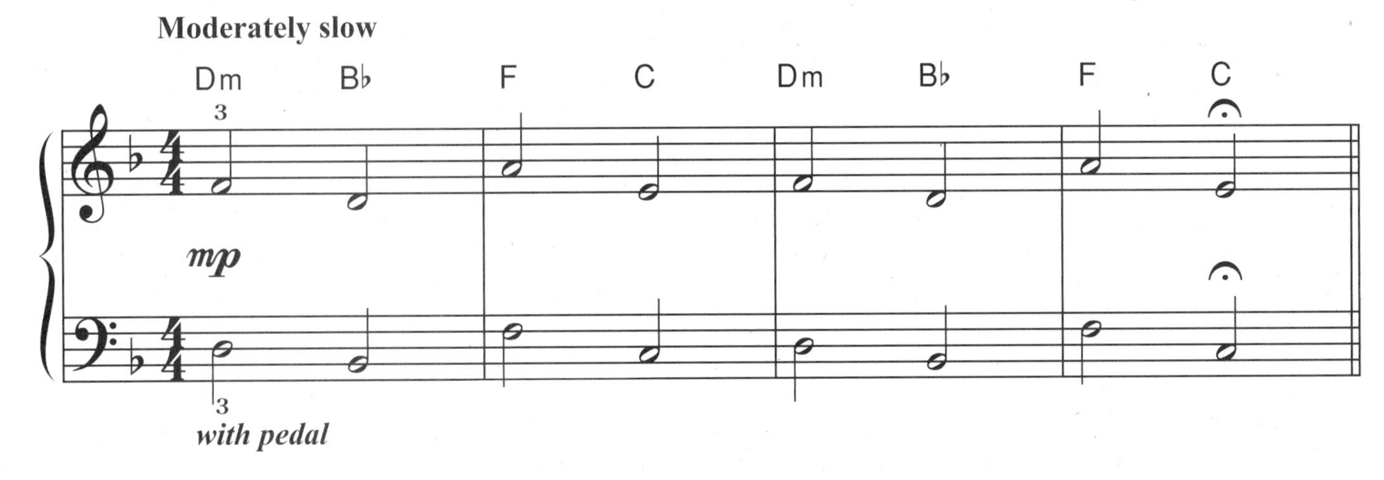

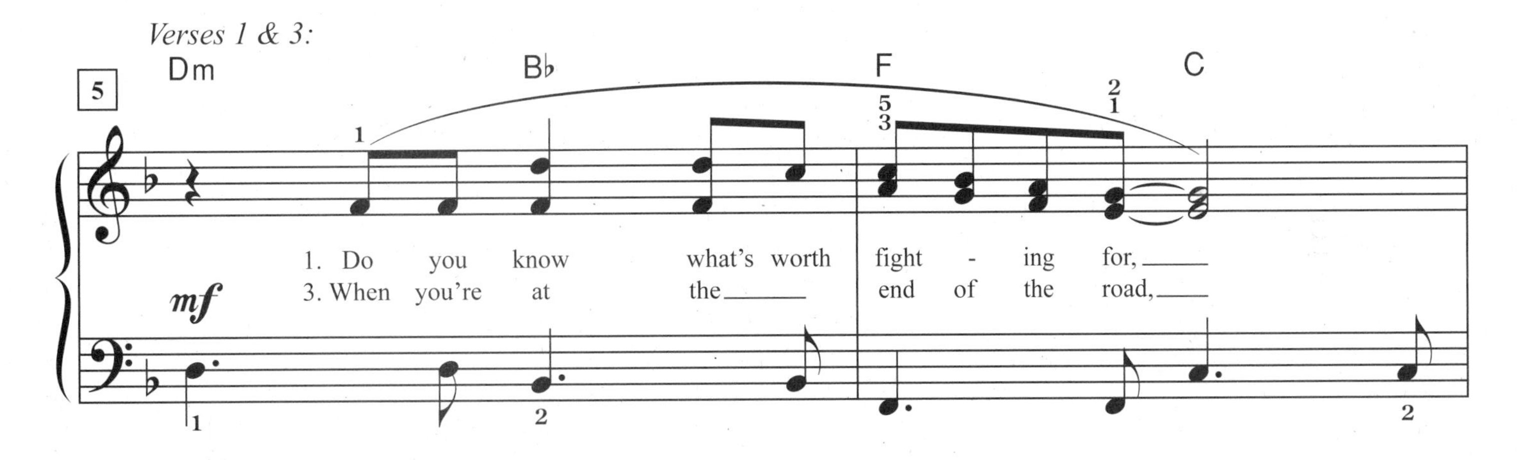

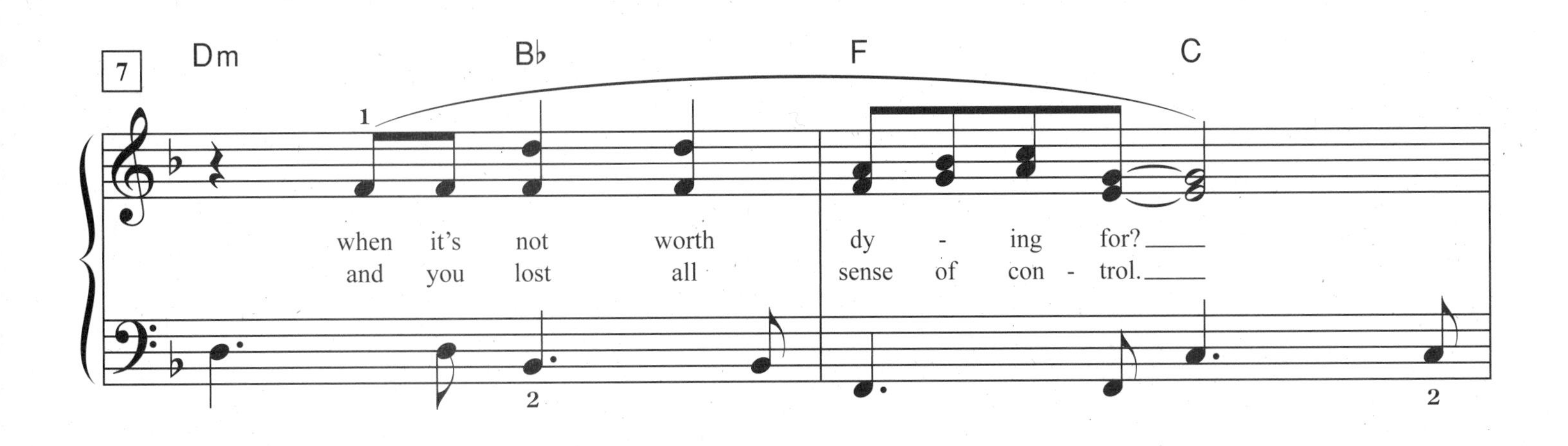

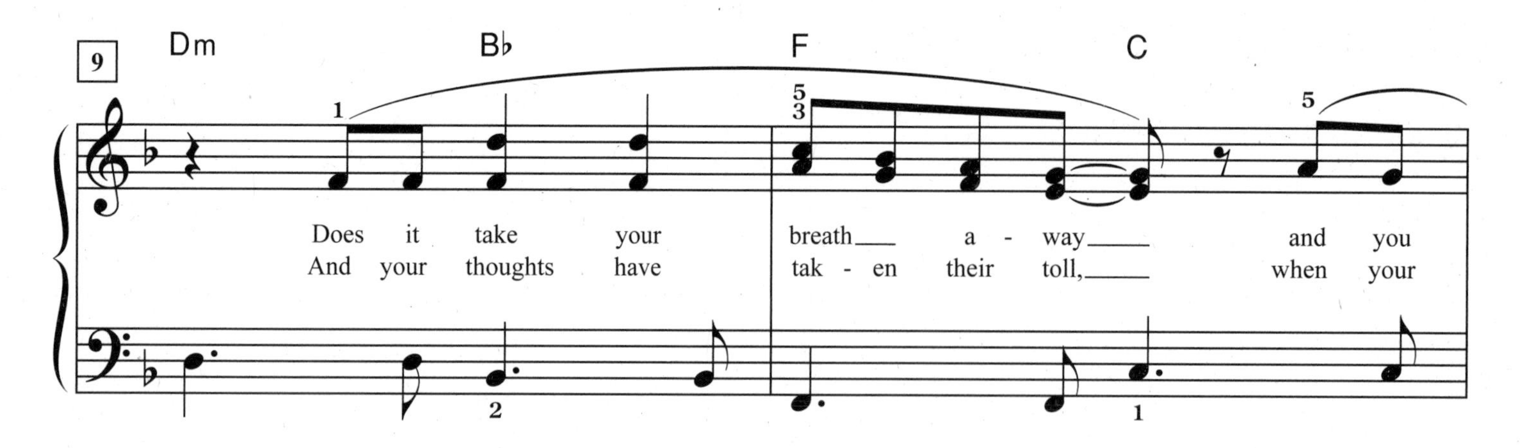

9
Dm
B♭
F
C
Does it take your breath a - way and you
And your thoughts have tak - en their toll, when your

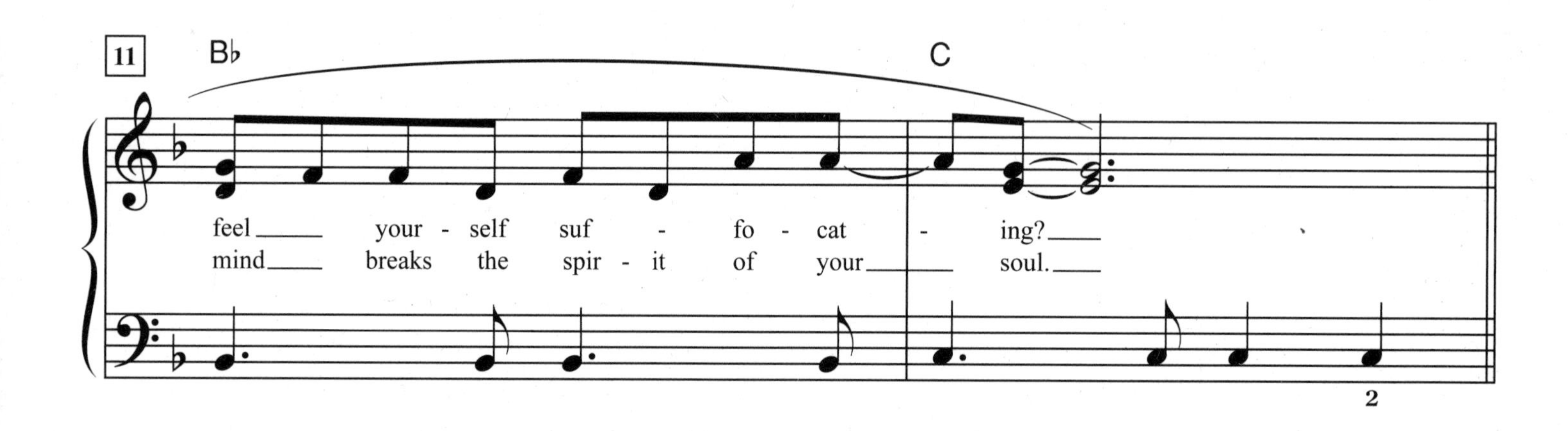

11
B♭
C
feel your - self suf - fo - cat - ing?
mind breaks the spir - it of your soul.

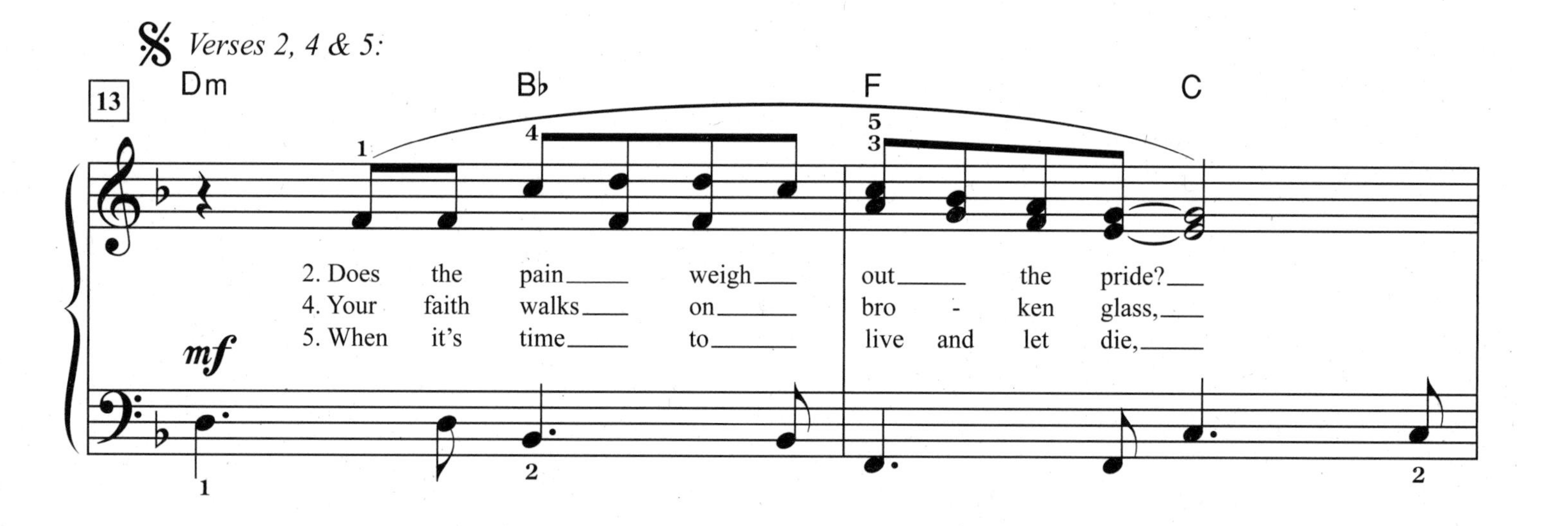

Verses 2, 4 & 5:
13
Dm
B♭
F
C
2. Does the pain weigh out the pride?
4. Your faith walks on bro - ken glass,
5. When it's time to live and let die,
mf

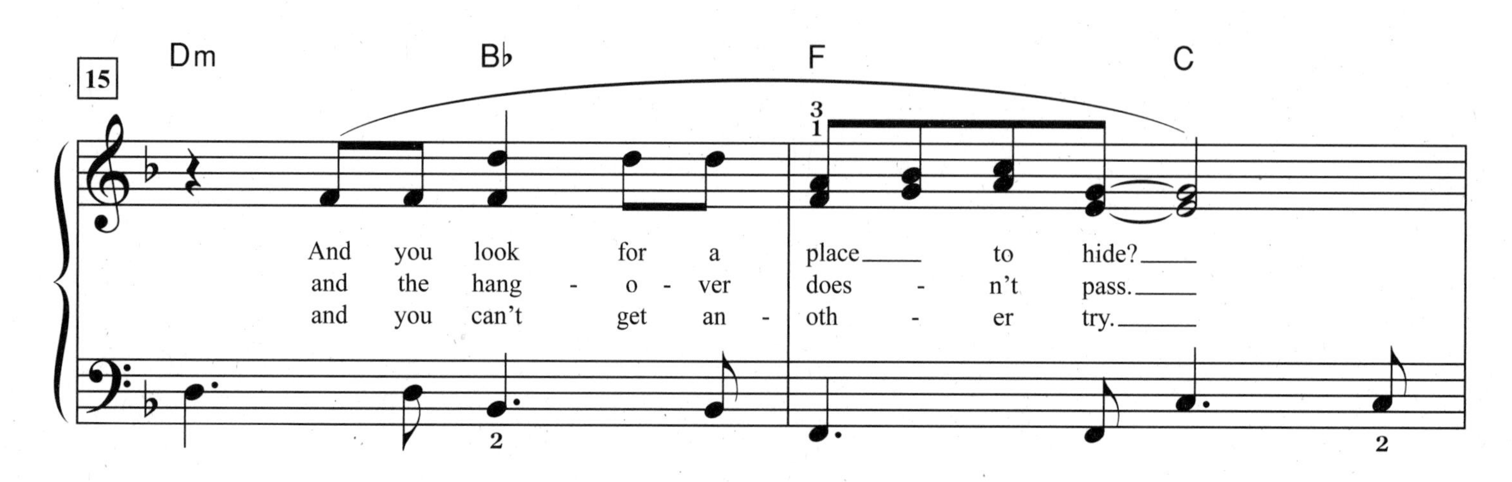

15
Dm
B♭
F
C
And you look for a place to hide?
and the hang - o - ver does - n't pass.
and you can't get an - oth - er try.

17
Dm
B♭
F
C
Did some - one break your heart in - side? You're in
Noth - ing's ev - er built to last. You're in
Some - thing in - side this heart has died. You're in

19
B♭
C
ru - ins.
ru - ins.
ru - ins.

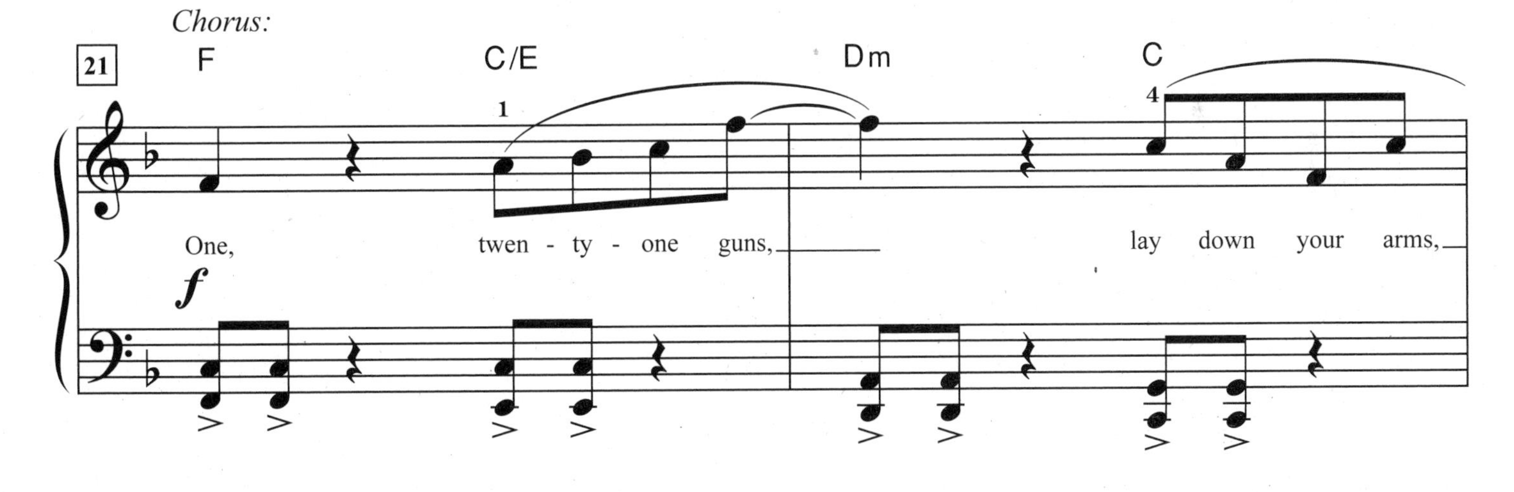
Chorus:
21
F
C/E
Dm
C
One, twen - ty - one guns, lay down your arms,
f

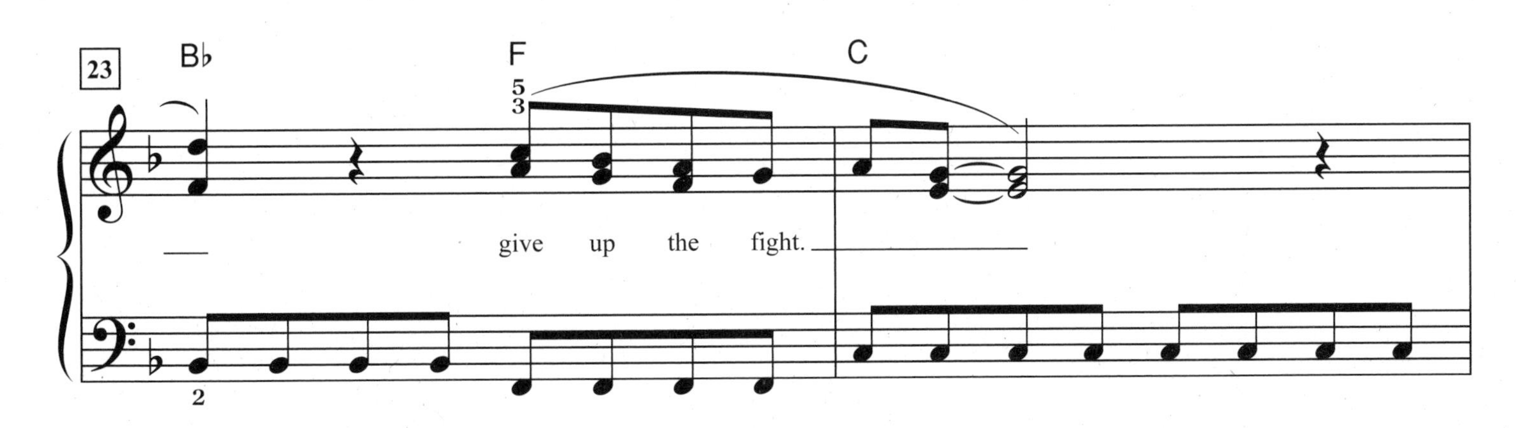
23
B♭
F
C
give up the fight.

to Coda
F C/E Dm C B♭ F
One, twen - ty - one guns, throw up your arms in - to the sky,
C B♭ F C
1.
you and I.
mf
2.
Bridge:
C Dm B♭ F C
f
Did you try to live on your own
Dm B♭ F A Dm B♭
when you burned down the house and home?
Did you stand too

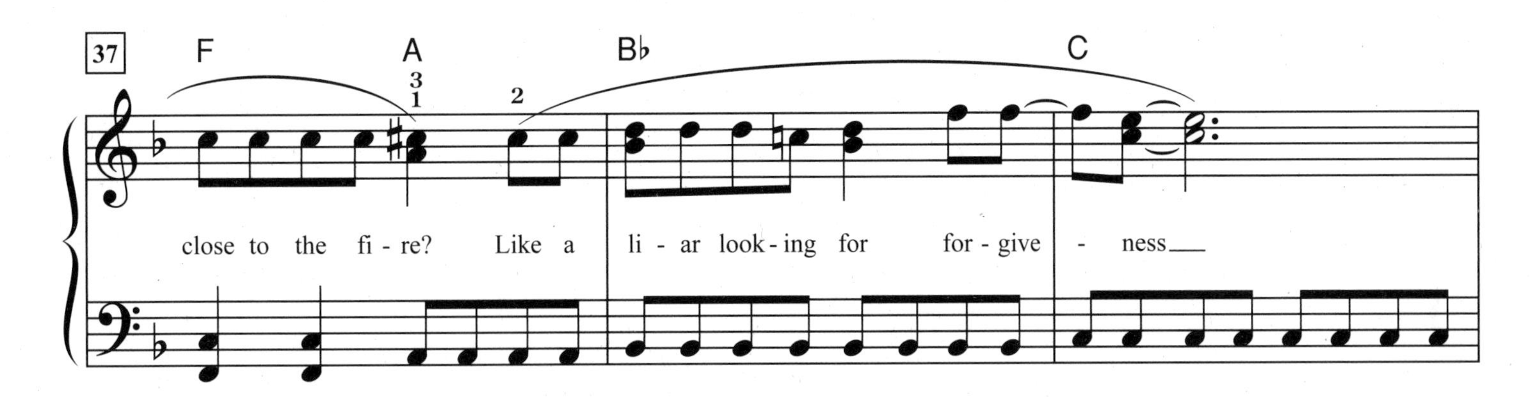
37
F
A
B♭
C
close to the fi - re? Like a
li - ar look - ing for for - give
- ness

D.S. al Coda
40
from a stone.

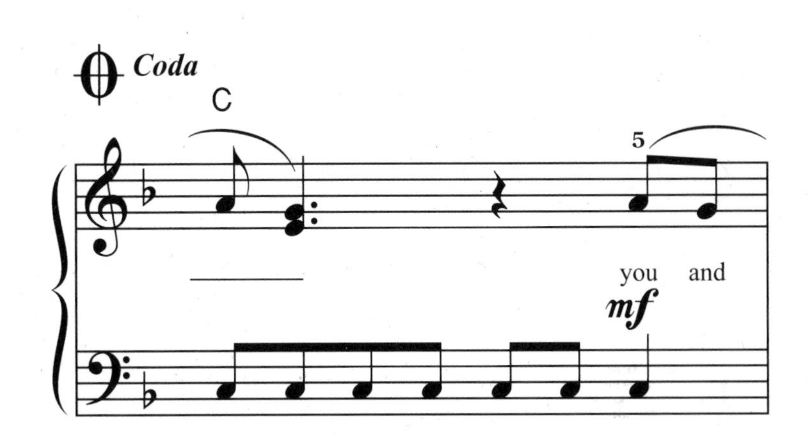
Coda
C
you and
mf

42
B♭
F
C
Freely
I.
No - bod - y likes you,
mp

45
ev - 'ry - one left you, they're
all out with - out you
hav - ing fun.

WAKE ME UP WHEN SEPTEMBER ENDS

Words by Billie Joe
Music by Green Day
Arranged by Carol Matz

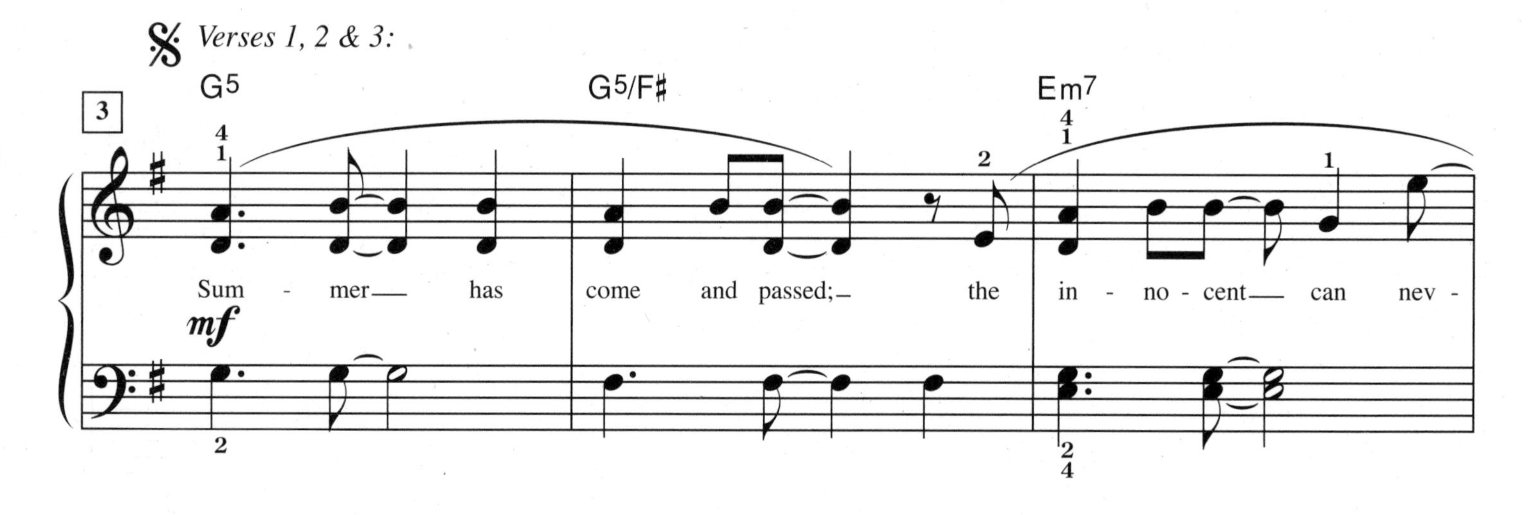

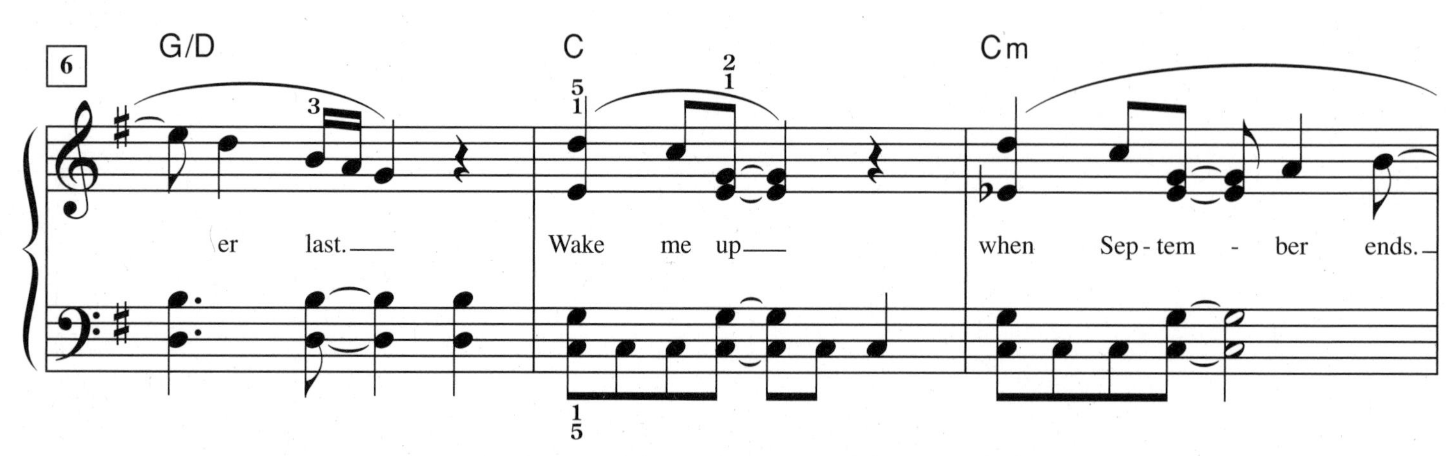

9
G5
Like my fa - ther's
Ring out the
Like my fa - ther's

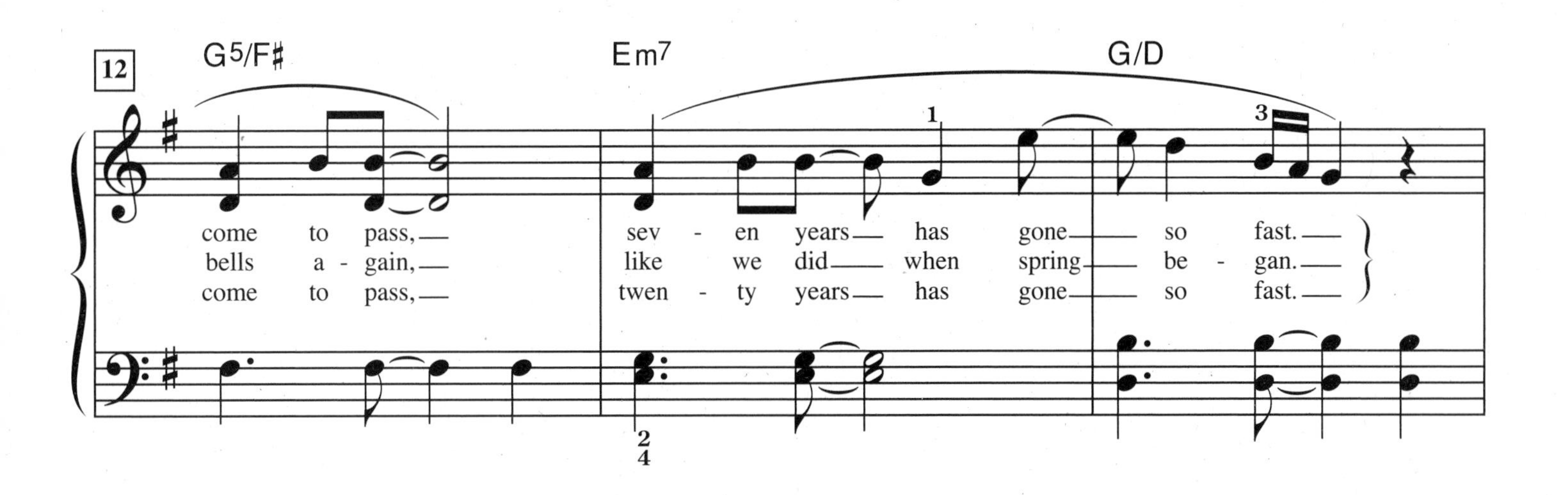
12
G5/F♯
Em7
G/D
come to pass, sev - en years has gone so fast.
bells a - gain, like we did when spring be - gan.
come to pass, twen - ty years has gone so fast.

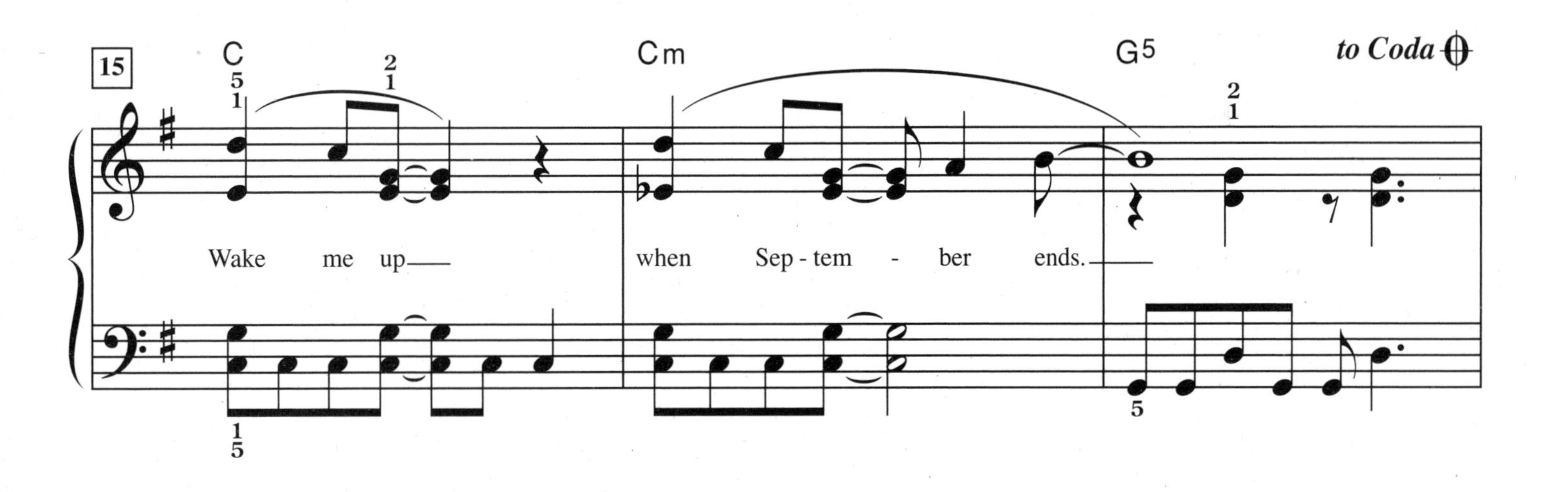
15
C
Cm
G5
to Coda
Wake me up when Sep - tem - ber ends.

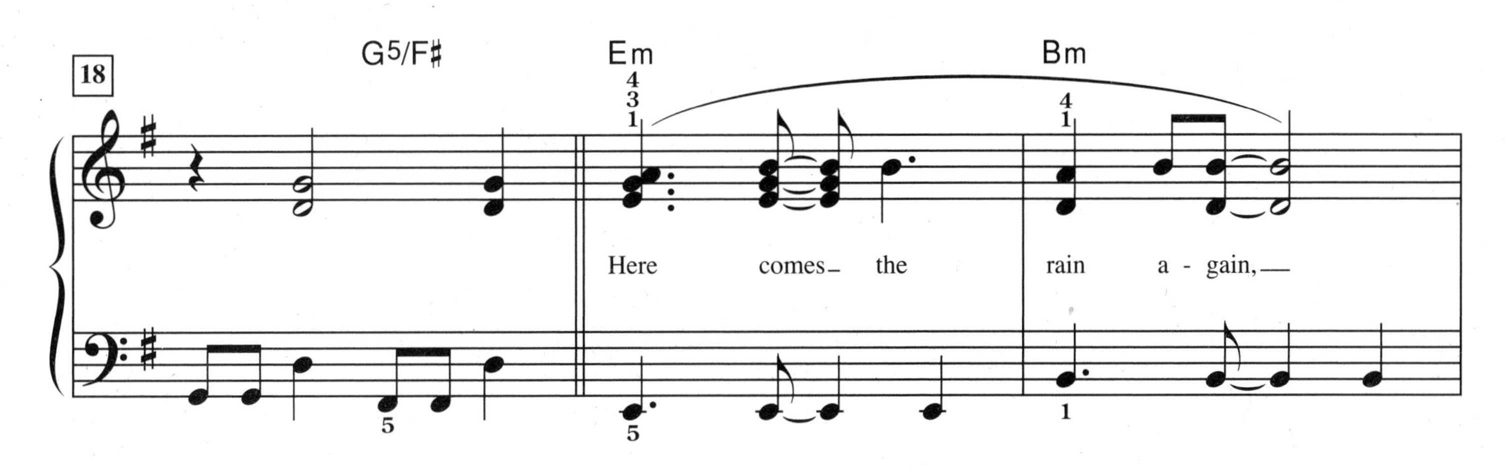
18
G5/F♯
Em
Bm
Here comes the rain a - gain,

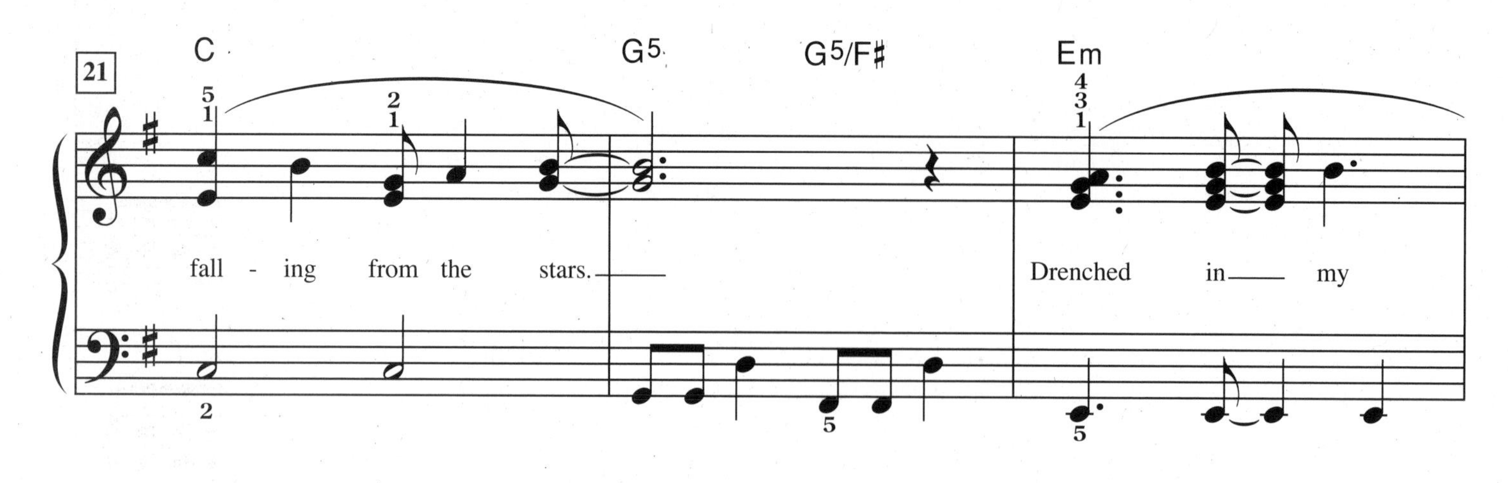

21
C
G5
G5/F♯
Em
fall - ing from the stars.
Drenched in my

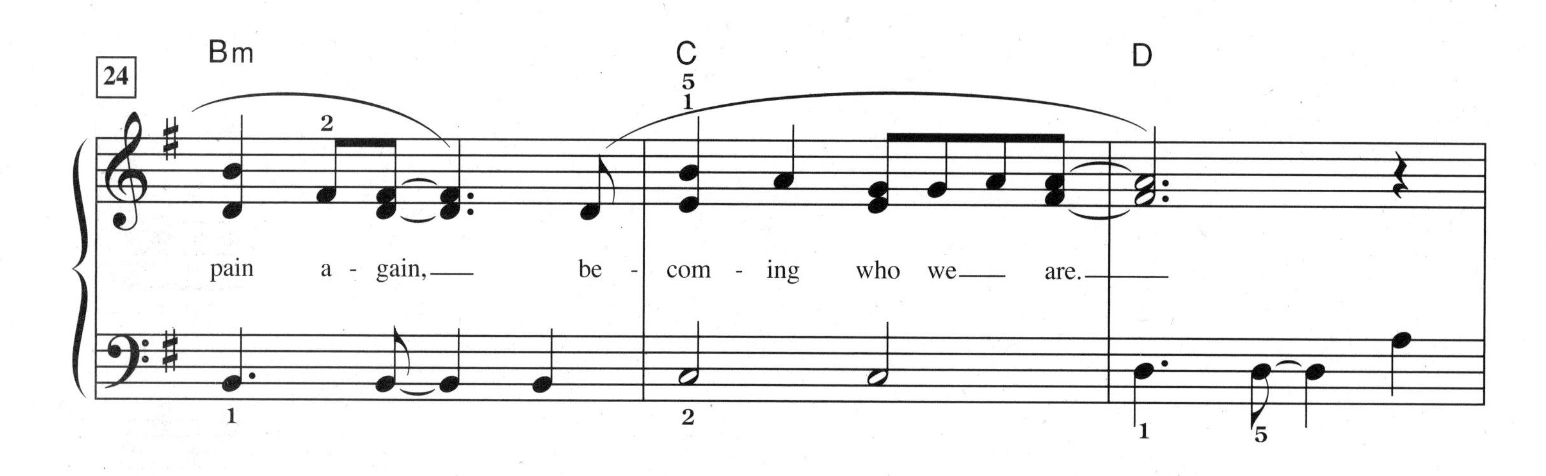

24
Bm
C
D
pain a - gain, be - com - ing who we are.

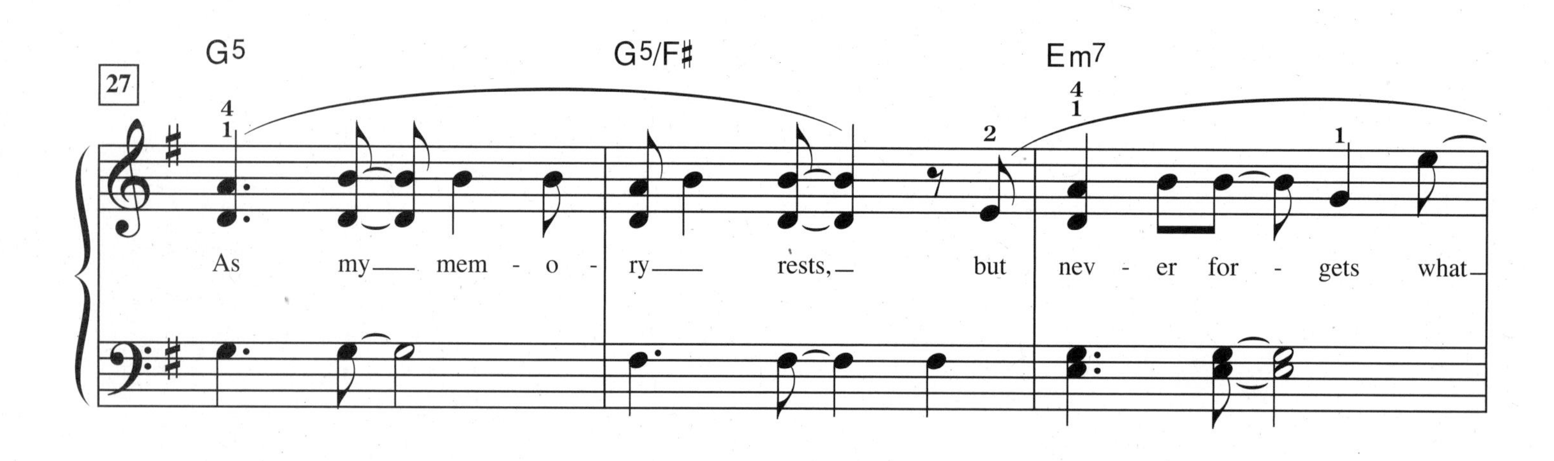

27
G5
G5/F♯
Em7
As my mem - o - ry rests, but nev - er for - gets what

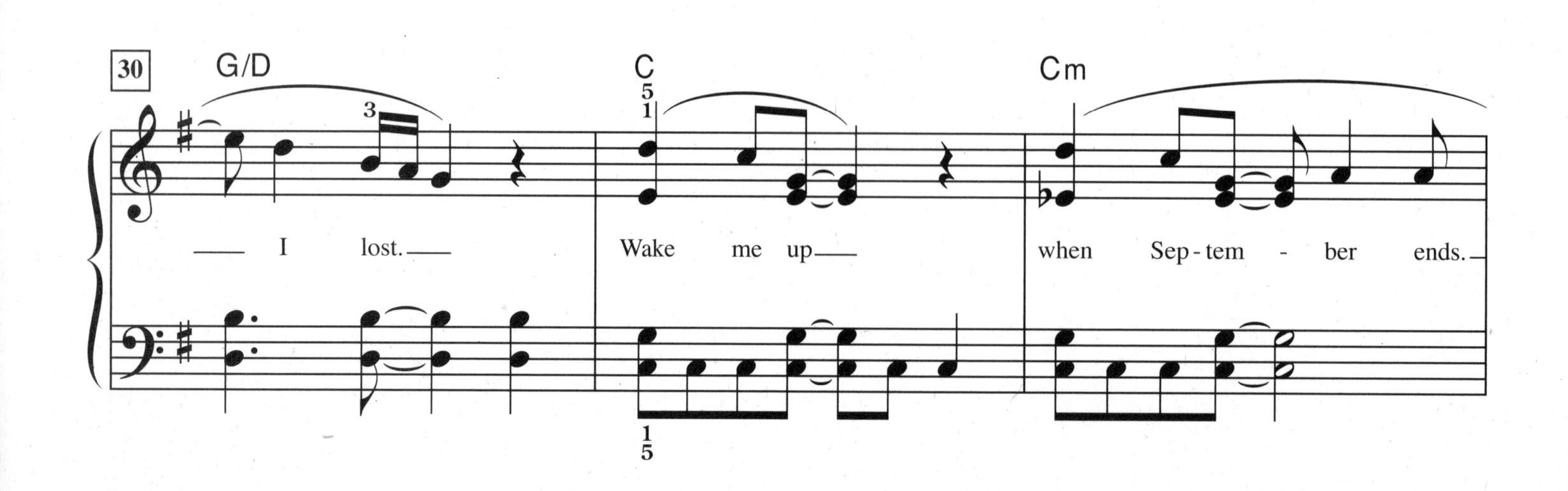

30
G/D
C
Cm
I lost. Wake me up when Sep - tem - ber ends.

33
G5
1.
37
2.
Instrumental:
G5
G5/F♯
Em
Bm
f
41
C
G5
D/F♯
Em
Bm

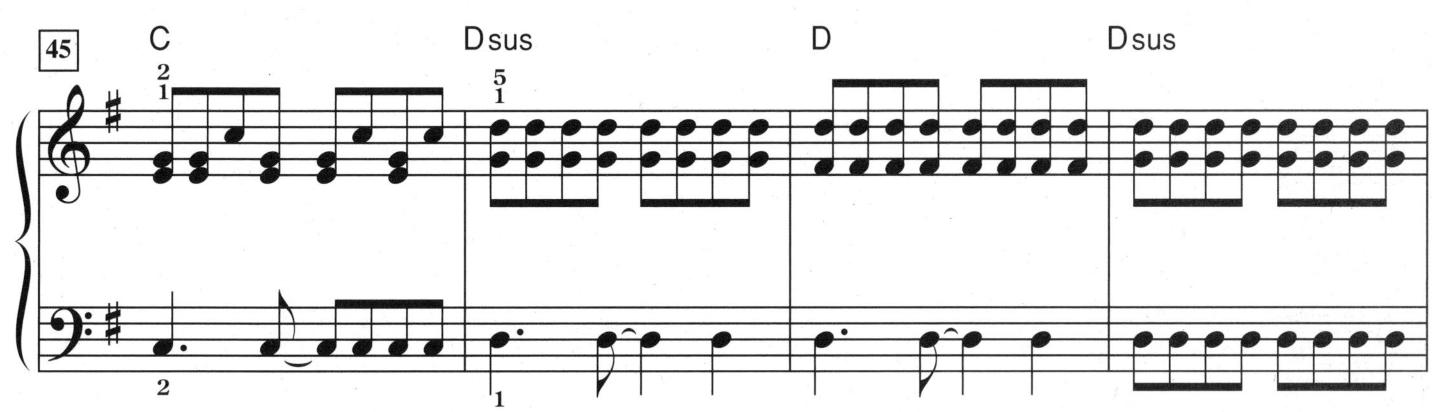
45
C
Dsus
D
Dsus

49
D
G5
mf
5
5
53
D.S. al Coda
Coda
G5
C
Wake me up
1
5

56
Cm
G5
2
1
when Sep - tem - ber ends.

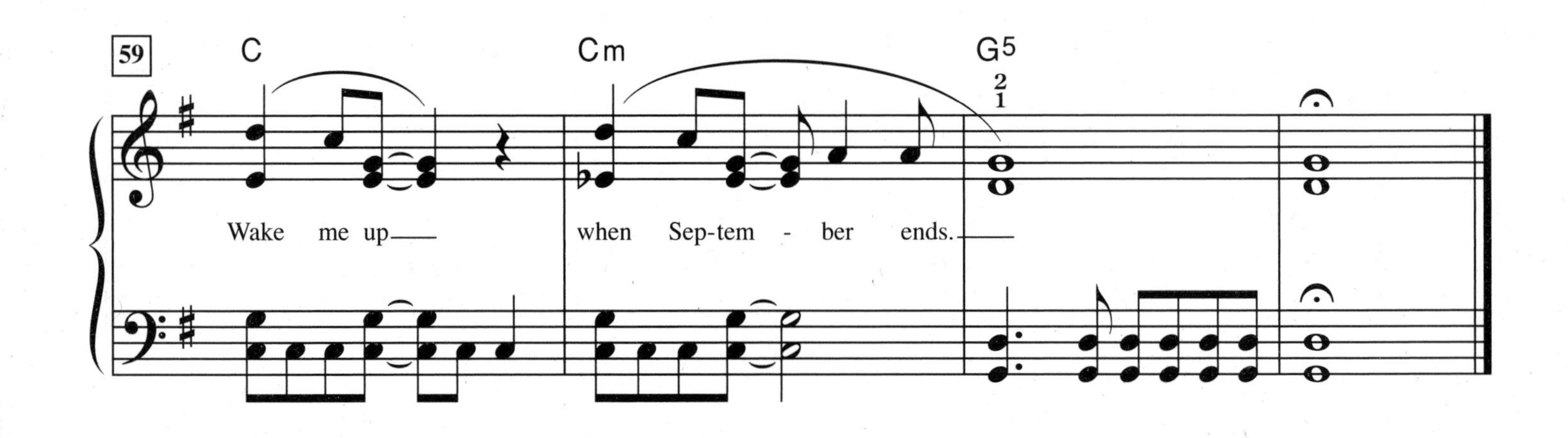
59
C
Cm
G5
2
1
Wake me up
when Sep-tem - ber ends.

WHATSERNAME

Words by Billie Joe
Music by Green Day
Arranged by Carol Matz

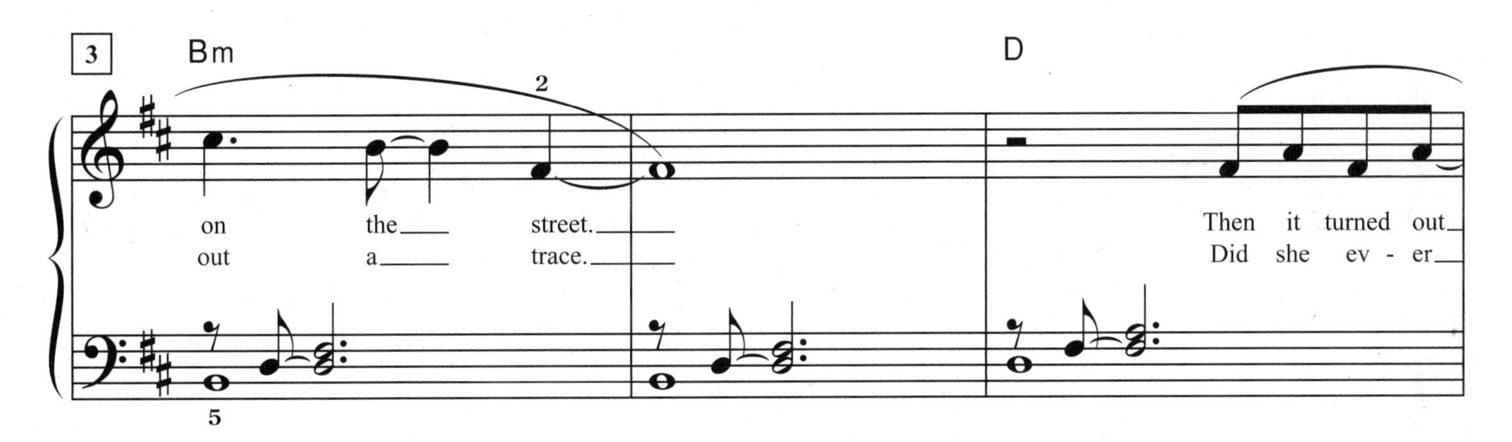

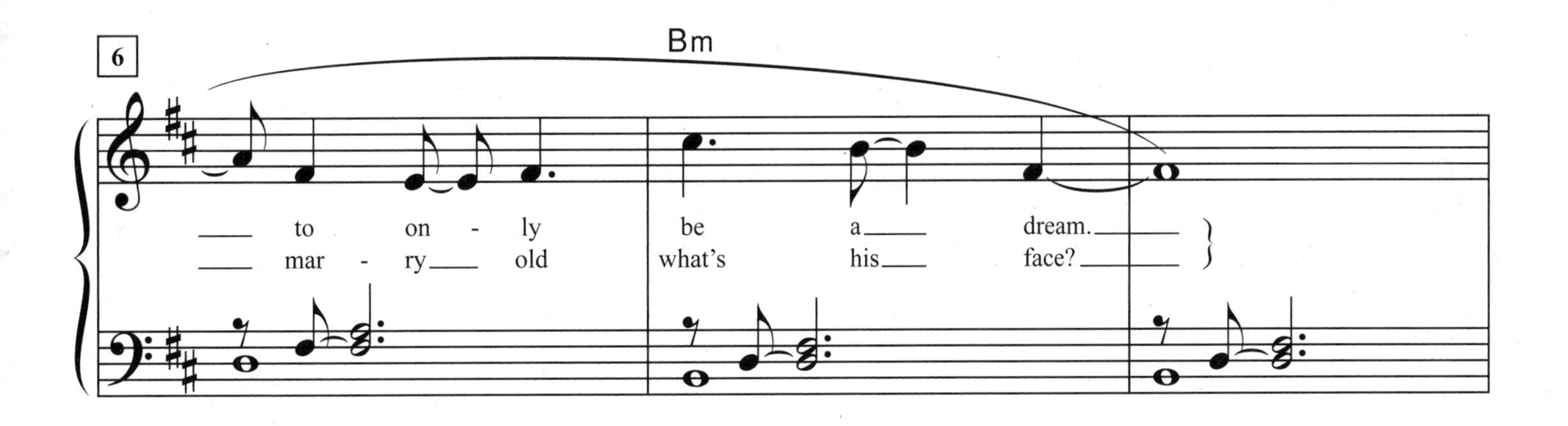

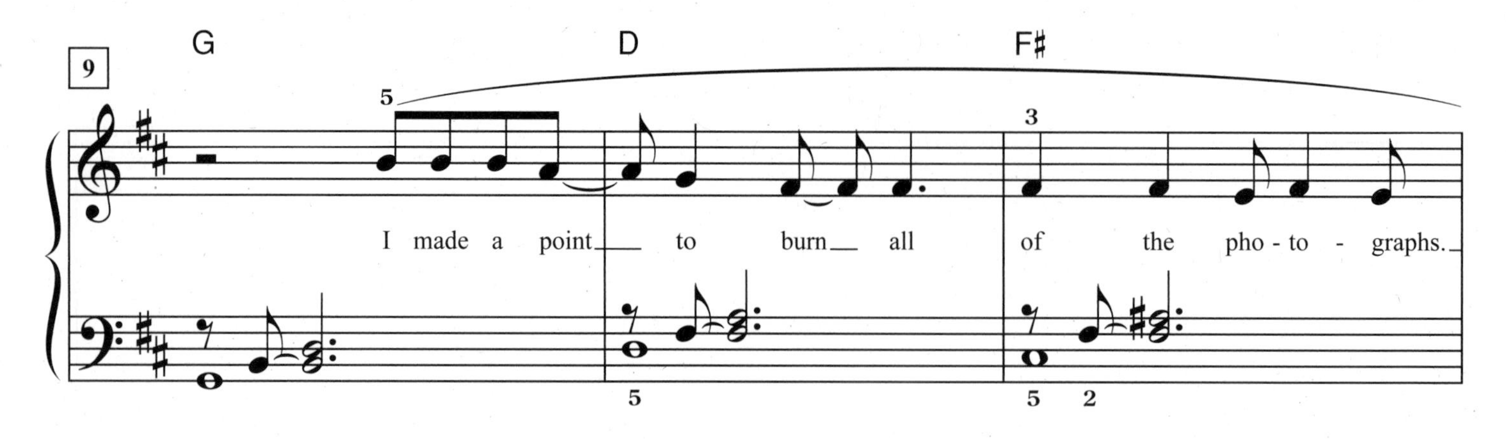
9
G
D
F♯
I made a point to burn all of the pho - to - graphs.

12
Bm
D/A
G
D
She went a - way and then I

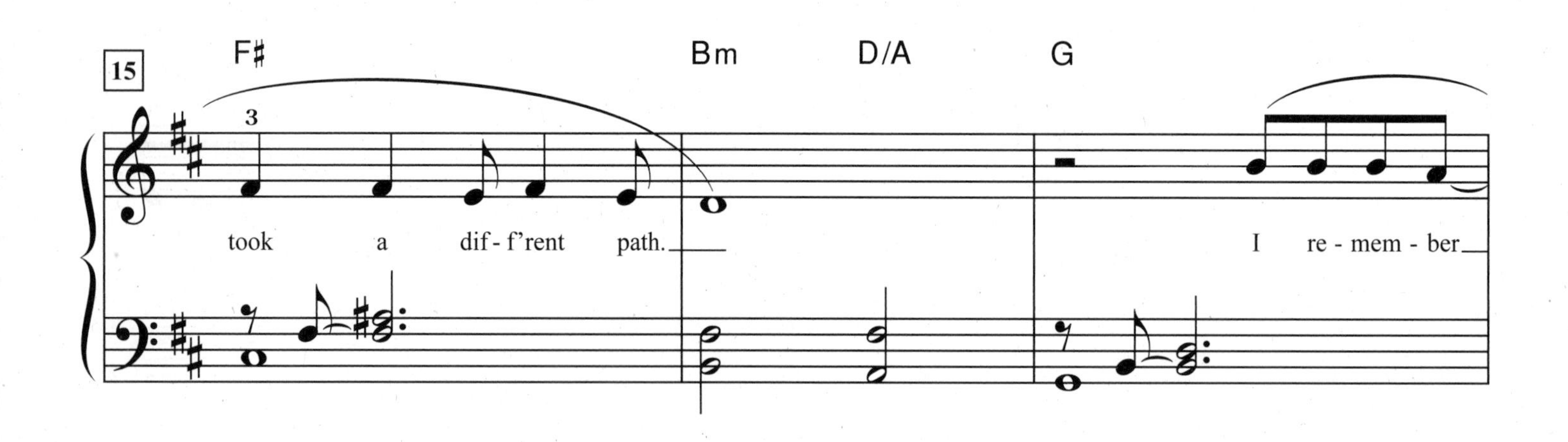
15
F♯
Bm
D/A
G
took a dif - f'rent path.
I re - mem - ber

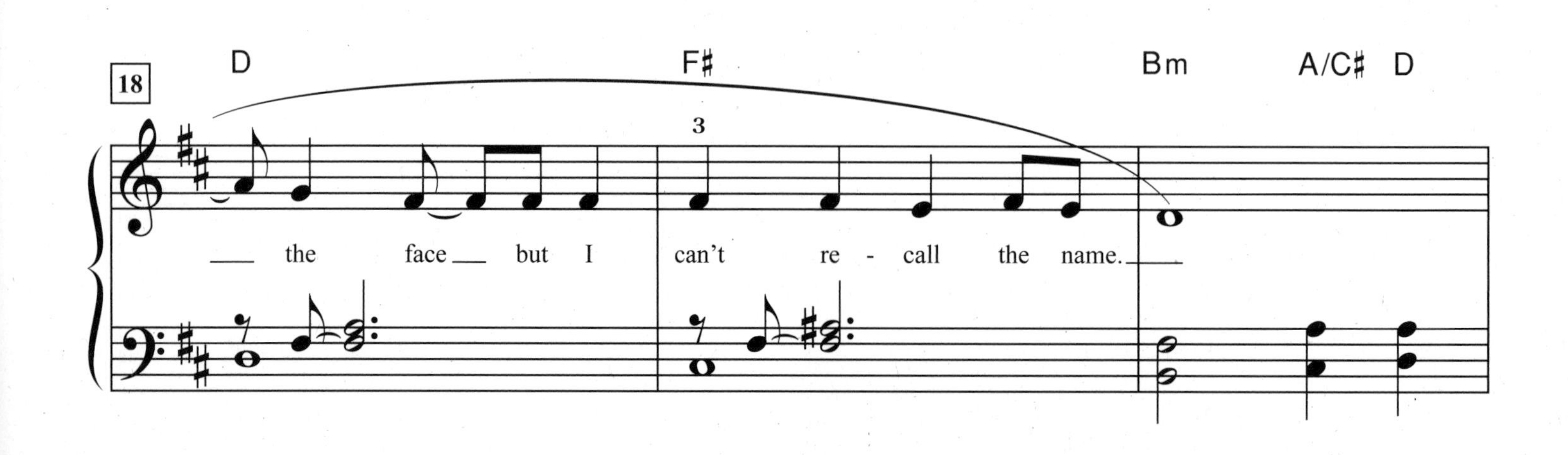
18
D
F♯
Bm
A/C♯
D
the face but I can't re - call the name.

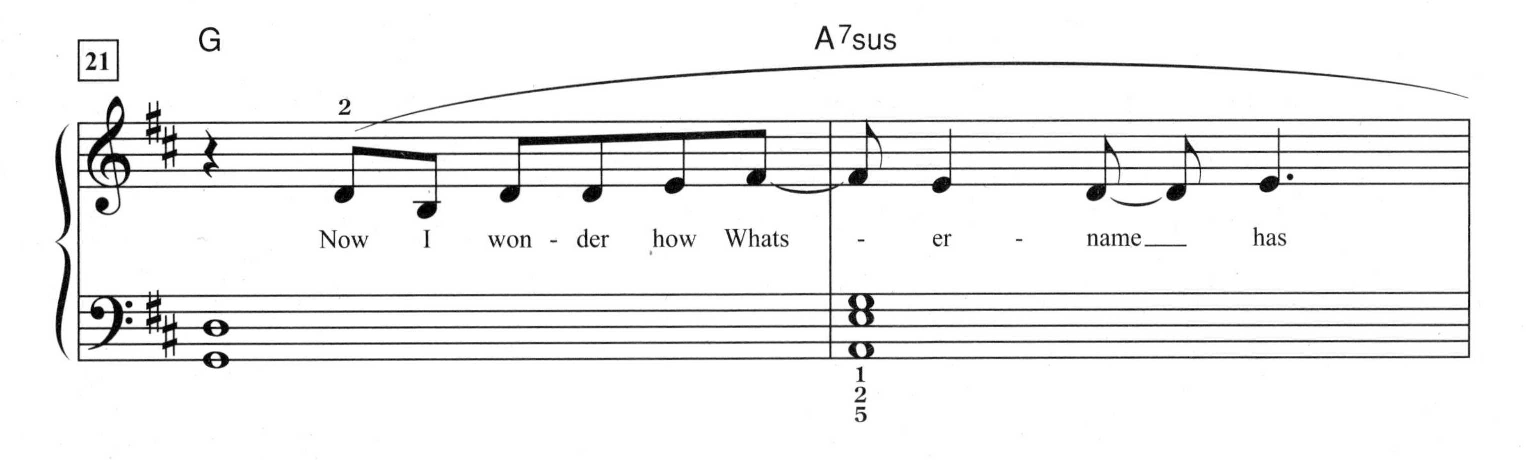
21
G
A7sus
Now I won - der how Whats - er - name has

23
1.
Dsus2
Bm7
been.

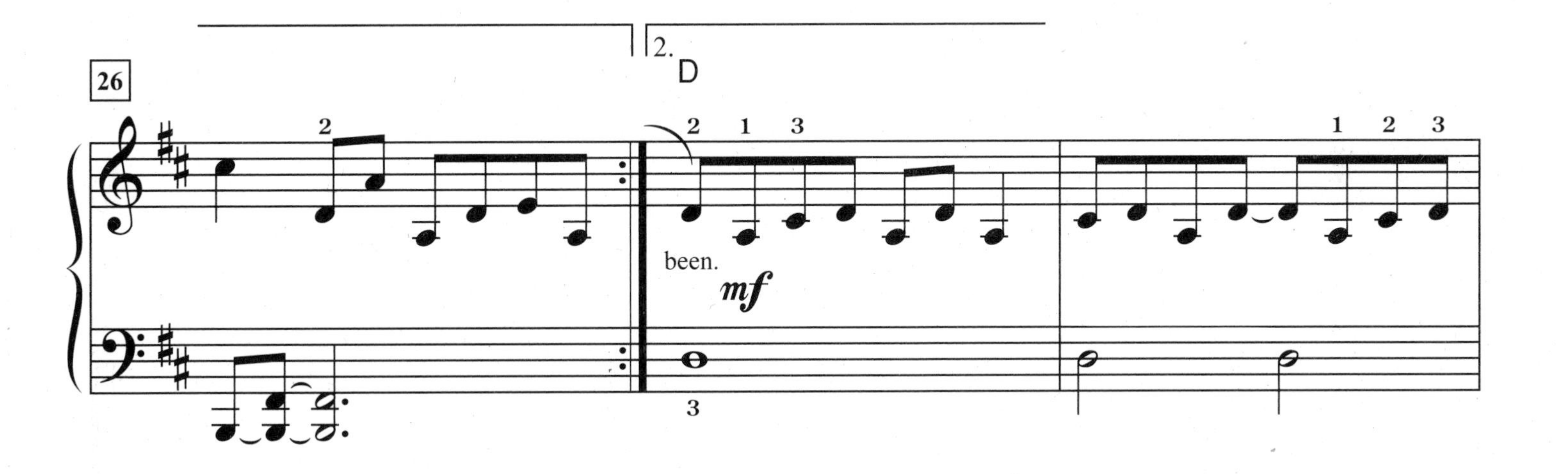
26
2.
D
been.
mf

29
Bsus2

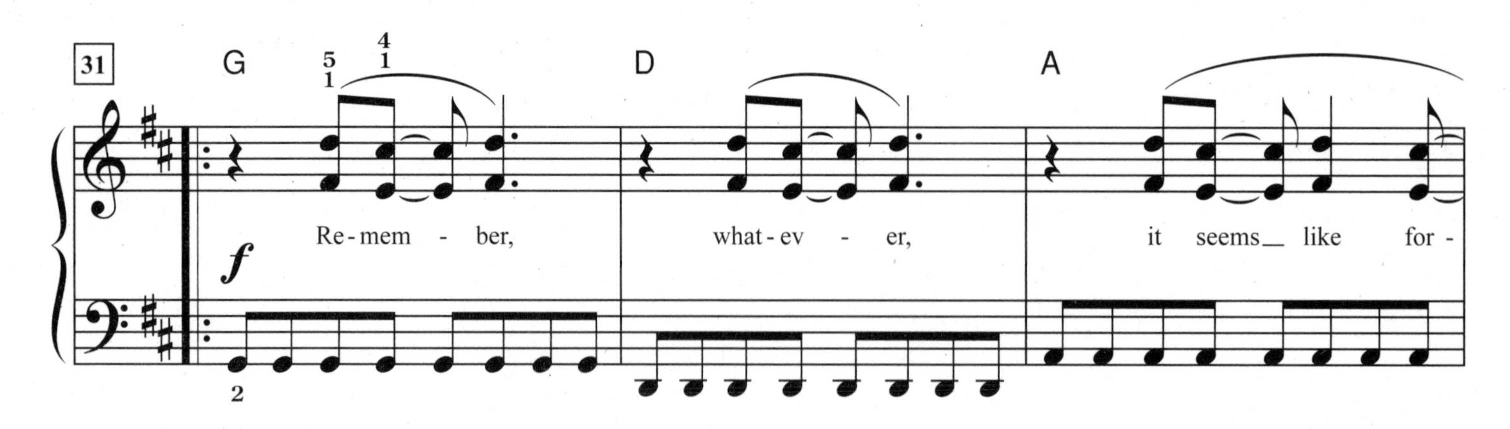
31
G
D
A
Re-mem - ber,
what-ev - er,
it seems_ like for -

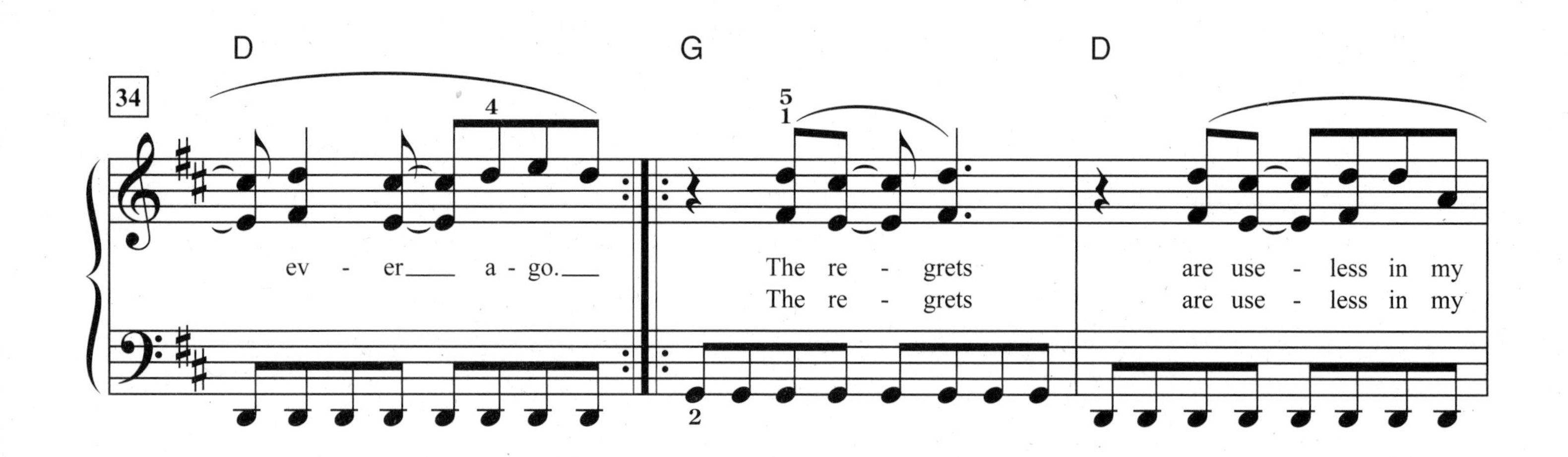
34
D
G
D
ev - er___ a - go.___
The re - grets
The re - grets
are use - less in my
are use - less in my

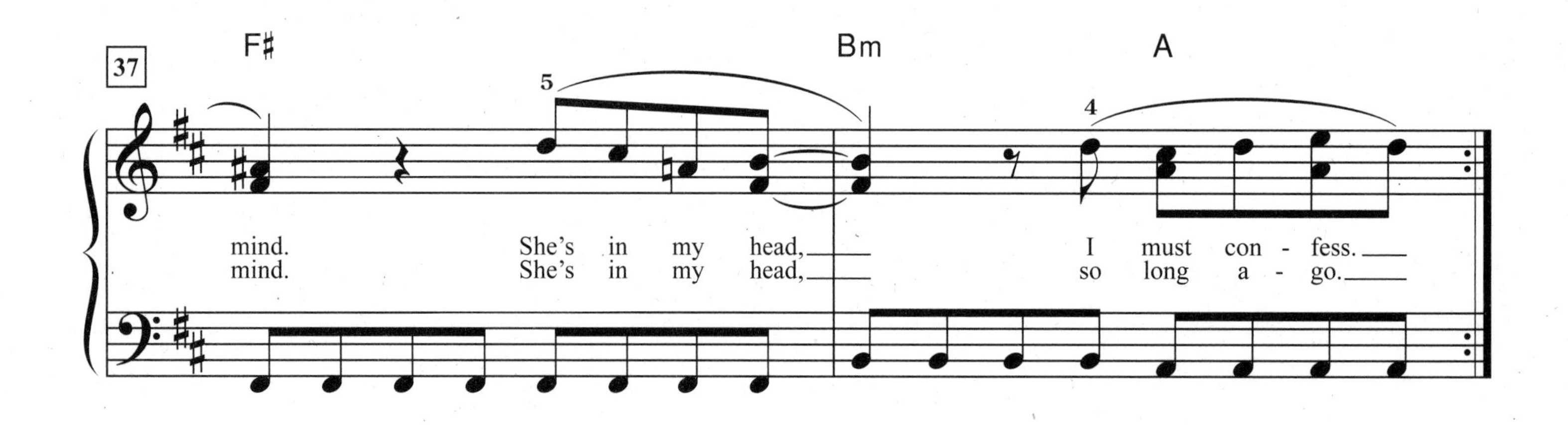
37
F♯
Bm
A
mind.
mind.
She's in my head,___
She's in my head,___
I must con - fess.___
so long a - go.___

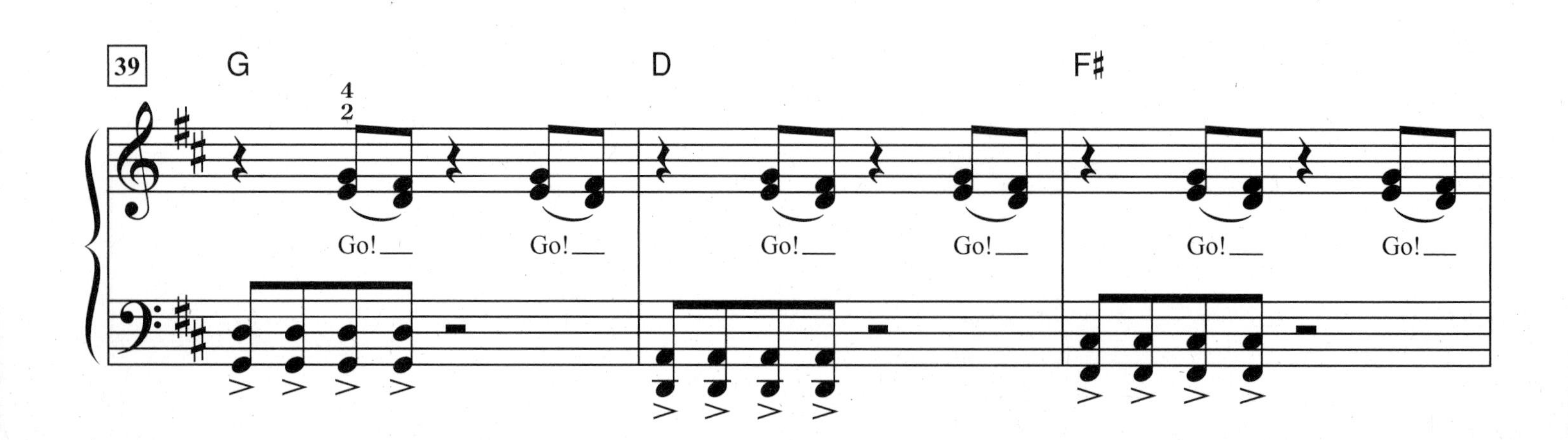
39
G
D
F♯
Go!__ Go!__
Go!__ Go!__
Go!__ Go!__

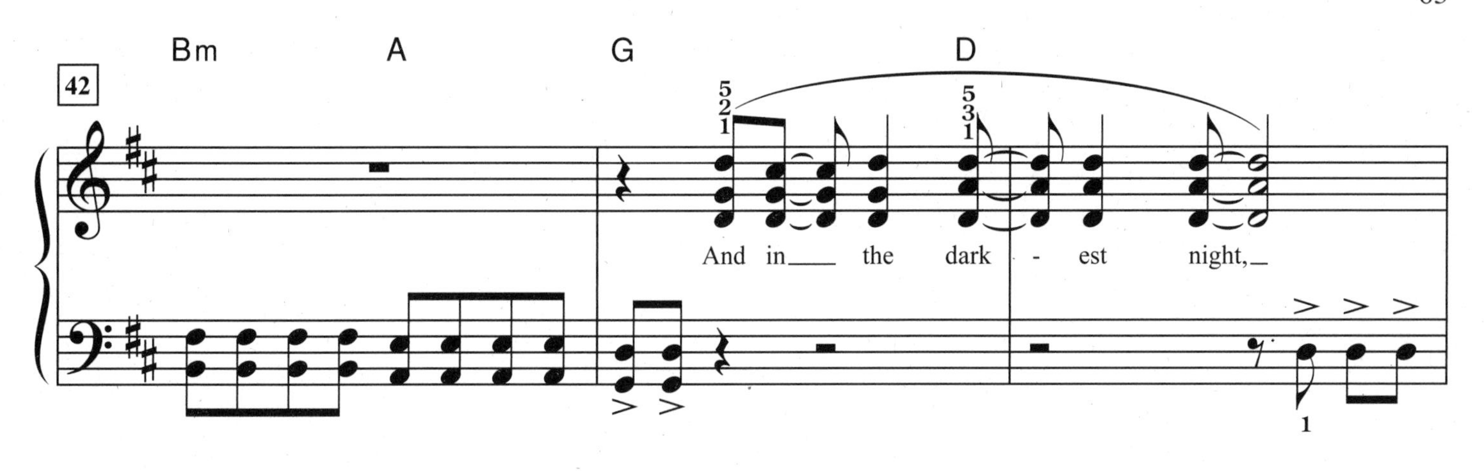
42
Bm A G D
And in the dark - est night,

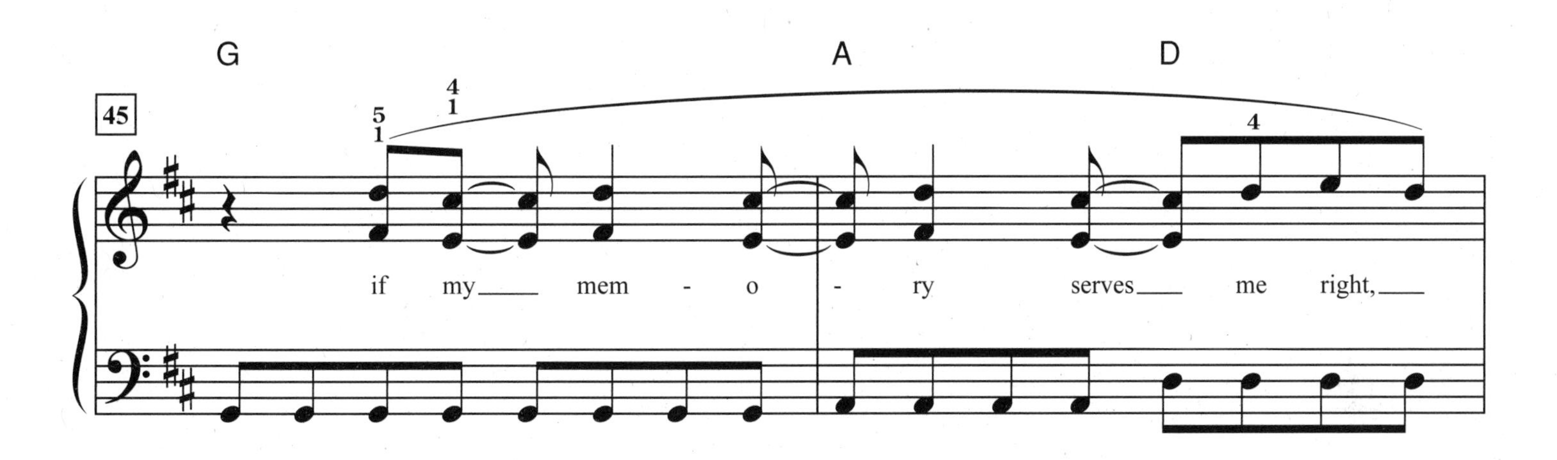
45
G A D
if my mem - o - ry serves me right,

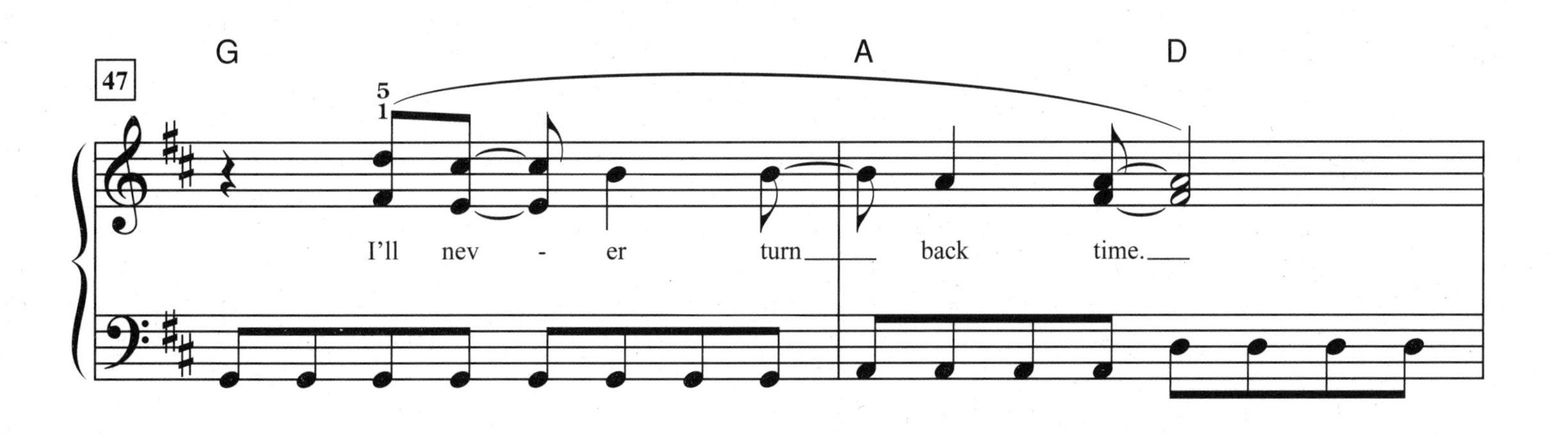
47
G A D
I'll nev - er turn back time.

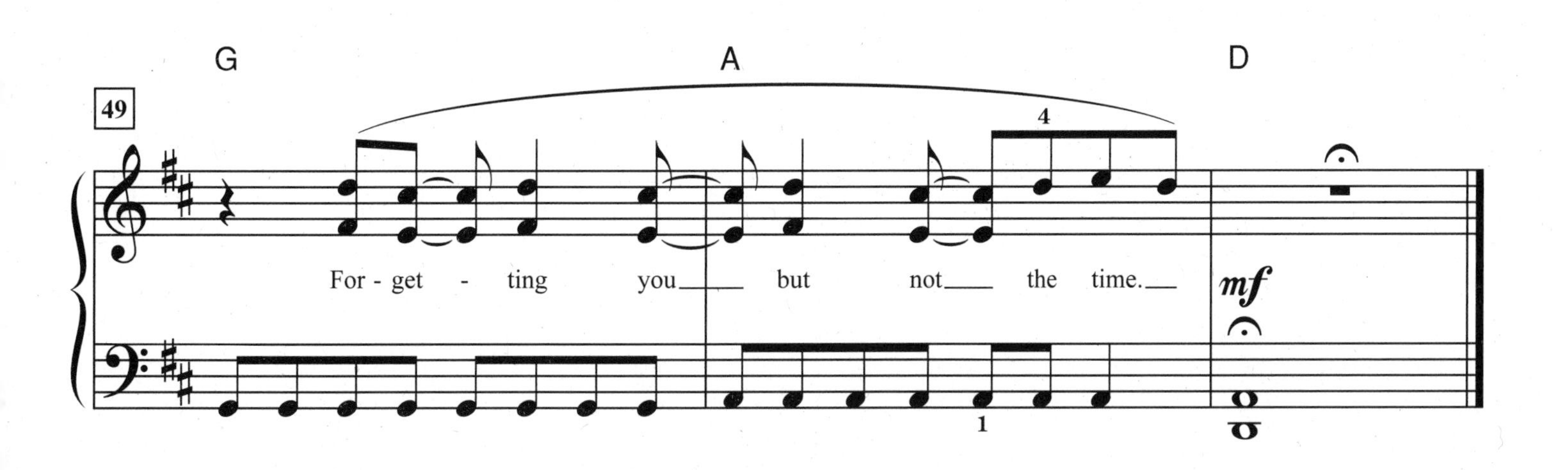
49
G A D
For - get - ting you but not the time.
mf

THUNDERS
& THE HEARTBREAKERS
NUNS CRIME
HATRED SURGE
ISHBONE
BANG DATA
WANTED
FOUR MORE
WARS!
DEAD
KENNEDYS